FLORIDA'S COAST-TO-COAST TRAIL GUIDE

FLORIDA'S COAST-TO-COAST TRAIL GUIDE

250-Miles of C2C Bicycle Rides and Walks— Titusville to St. Petersburg

NANCI ADLER

Palm Beach, Florida

Pineapple Press

An imprint of Globe Pequot, the trade division of
The Rowman & Littlefield Publishing Group, Inc.
4501 Forbes Blvd., Ste. 200
Lanham, MD 20706
www.rowman.com

Distributed by NATIONAL BOOK NETWORK

British Library Cataloguing in Publication Information available

Library of Congress Cataloging-in-Publication Data available
ISBN 978-1-68334-319-6 (paper : alk. PB)
ISBN 978-1-68334-320-2 (electronic)

♾™ The paper used in this publication meets the minimum requirements of American National Standard for Information Sciences—Permanence of Paper for Printed Library Materials, ANSI/NISO Z39.48-1992.

DISCLAIMER

None of the routes mentioned in this book were developed by the author, and some of them share public roads or intersections with cars and trucks. Route decisions should be made based on the conditions at the time of travel and the fitness and experience of the rider or walker. Cycling is an inherently dangerous activity. No guarantees are made as to the safety of any route.

CONTENTS

Introduction: The Florida Coast-to-Coast Trail
and the Focus of This Book 1

Know Before You Go 5

Florida's Heritage Along the C2C Path 11

Trail Section 1
Titusville to Osteen—*30 miles* 17
    (& optional spur to New Smyrna Beach)

Trail Section 2
Osteen to Sanford Wayside Park—*13 miles* 36
    (& optional spur on the Spring to Spring Trail)

Trail Section 3
Sanford Wayside Park to Altamonte Springs—*17 miles* . . 55
    (& optional spur to Sanford town center)

Trail Section 4
Altamonte Springs to Clermont—*31 miles* 70

Trail Section 5
Clermont to Spring Hill Trailhead—*55 miles** 87
    Mileage when trail is complete, projected 2026

Trail Section 6
Spring Hill Trailhead to Tarpon Springs—*47 miles* 105

Contents

Trail Section 7

Tarpon Springs to Clearwater—*14 miles* 118
(& optional spurs to Honeymoon Island and
Clearwater Beach)

Trail Section 8

Clearwater to St. Petersburg—*22 miles* 138

Practical Planning: Suggested Itineraries and Resources. . . 153

Appendix: Crossing the Gap Between Groveland and
Brooksville (in Trail Section 5). 162

Sources and References 165

Index 167

Acknowledgments 180

About the Author 181

About the Photographer 182

Overview

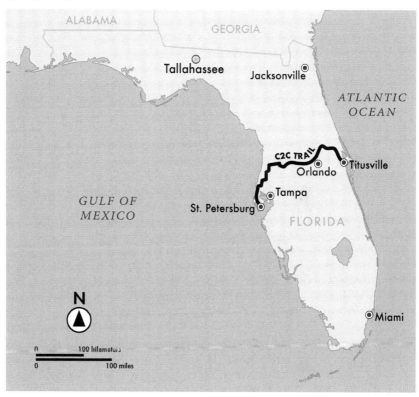

Florida's Coast-to-Coast Trail, connecting the Atlantic Ocean to the Gulf of Mexico

C2C Trail

Full length of the C2C from Titusville to St. Petersburg

INTRODUCTION: THE FLORIDA COAST-TO-COAST TRAIL AND THE FOCUS OF THIS BOOK

Bicycling and walking are ideal ways to discover and explore the outdoors. You can immerse yourself in the experience, savor unspoiled natural areas, and meet and engage with other people in small towns that are rich in culture and history. The intentional pace of cycling or walking allows you to fully absorb your surroundings. As an added benefit, these methods of travel offer exercise and plenty of fresh air. In Florida, one of the best ways to experience the central region of the state is to literally get off the beaten track, away from the high-volume tourist attractions, and explore the state's Coast-to-Coast Trail.

The Florida Coast-to-Coast Trail, or C2C, is a nearly 250-mile paved route that crosses the state from the Atlantic coast to the Gulf of Mexico, connecting Titusville to St. Petersburg.[1] Cyclists and walkers can use this route to take advantage of Florida's mild winters, plentiful sunshine, and relatively flat geography. Whether you choose to explore the entire length of the C2C Trail or to simply discover some of the trail's highlights, I want to share with you some insight and background for your travels.

---

1. At the time of publication, the 11-mile extension of the C2C east of Titusville to the beach is still in the planning phase. There are two additional unfinished segments: a 5-mile gap in Orange County (sidewalks can be used here) and a 28-plus-mile gap between Groveland and Brooksville. The Groveland to Brooksville gap is addressed in the Appendix.

The C2C connects existing regional paved trails, including the lengthy Pinellas Trail (opened in 1990) and the scenic Seminole Wekiva Trail (opened in 2000). Planners used existing infrastructure and worked to establish connections that would complete the coast-to-coast path. This piecemeal construction means that the trail signage can sometimes be confusing and inconsistent. Fortunately, signage is improving, and modern technology provides access to valuable online resources, such as GPS location and mapping information (e.g., Google Maps bicycle layer option), that make navigation much easier.

In this book, I will take you along the C2C heading east to west, starting in Titusville and ending in St. Petersburg. I chose this direction for one primary reason: there are multiple lodging, dining, and entertainment opportunities in St. Petersburg, which will tempt you to stay overnight and savor the end of a coast-to-coast trip. Obviously, heading west to east works well, too, so the chapters in this book are organized by trail segments, allowing you to refer to the chapter relating to the trail segment you are traveling.

Each chapter focuses on a geographic trail segment, with mileage noted at the beginning of the chapter. The eight trail section chapters are not based on mileage but rather on the volume of information necessary to give readers a good perspective of the section through which they are traveling. Trail users should plan their daily trip mileage based on their personal preferences and capabilities. Suggested itineraries are provided in a later chapter of this book and take into account lodging availability.

While the C2C is generally thought of as a long-distance bicycling route because of its impressive length, it is equally suited for walking. Walkers can enjoy portions of the route for a short stroll or a multiday, long-distance adventure. Although you can walk the trail's entire paved path, some sections are more enjoyable for walking because of their scenic beauty. Other factors include shade cover, avoiding motorized traffic, and distances between trailheads. With these considerations in mind, I include recommended walks in each trail section's chapter.

2

A chilly January morning out on the C2C along the Seminole Wekiva Trail segment

This companion guide is not a mile-by-mile how-to guide, nor does it provide extensive details about lodging, camping, or restaurants. Since much of that information changes frequently, the most up-to-date source is the internet. Instead, I focus on interesting cultural and natural aspects of the route—the places to go and things to see that cyclists and walkers will enjoy as they travel across central Florida. By highlighting the local flavor of small towns, the natural beauty of Florida, and the historical setting of the area, I want readers to discover Florida's uniqueness and to fully appreciate the communities, both human and natural, through which they travel.

Exploring an area using a slower, more mindful mode of transportation provides unparalleled opportunities for discovery, reflection, and connection that are hard to achieve with car-centered travel. You increase your chances of interacting with locals, for seeing unusual animals, or for finding refreshments at an off-the-beaten path café or pub.

The C2C path takes you directly through the heart of four official "Trail Towns": Titusville, Winter Garden, Clermont, and Dunedin. These towns are designated by Florida's Office of Greenways and Trails based on many criteria. Trail Towns warmly welcome trail walkers and bicyclists, encourage them to explore the area, and offer amenities and information.

Many of the towns along the C2C are small. Consequently, the operating hours for local museums, heritage centers, and nature centers may be limited. Check websites for opening hours and admission information.

Whether you are riding or walking portions of the C2C, doing single-day excursions, embarking on a multiday cycling trip, or crossing the State of Florida on the entire C2C route, this book is for you. Knowing the distinctive localities through which you travel makes the experience richer and your enjoyment greater.

KNOW BEFORE YOU GO

Researching an unfamiliar region before exploring it will make the outing more successful and enjoyable. In addition to the cultural, historical, and natural environment information I provide in the following chapters, you'll want to think about details such as weather, lodging, safety, and logistics.

Keep in mind your own fitness level and weather conditions for your excursions, whether it is a morning jaunt or a multiday tour. Cycling 30 miles in 60-degree good weather is a very different experience than cycling 30 miles in 90-degree heat with a headwind.

Most of the Florida peninsula is in a subtropical climate, and summer days are hot and humid. Outdoor enthusiasts know to carry plenty of food and drink, especially water, while active during the hot months. During summers, it is best to begin your adventures in the morning before the heat builds up. An early start will also help avoid the frequent afternoon thunderstorms. Avoid strenuous physical activity during high temperatures if you are not acclimatized to the heat.

Winters in Florida are generally mild, subject to some chilly spells brought in from cold fronts that may bring rain. Autumn and spring can be variable but typically offer very pleasant conditions. You can undertake the C2C at any time of year, but I prefer the period from October to April for Florida bicycle tours and long-distance walks.

If you are traveling the entire length of the C2C, you may want to plan the overnight stops in advance to help make the trip successful. Availability of camping and hotel rooms will vary based on the season and day of the week.

Safety concerns are paramount for all cycling, walking, and hiking adventures. When using shared-use paths, be aware of your surroundings and stay alert. Children and pets on trails can be unpredictable, and other trail users may enter onto the path unexpectedly. Wearing brightly colored clothing will make you more visible to other trail users and motorists. The pedestrian and bicycle traffic on the C2C path varies tremendously. In some remote areas, there may be few others on the trail, while in towns like Dunedin and Winter Garden the trails are often full of activity, particularly on weekends.

The C2C travels through rural, suburban, residential, and commercial areas. Although crime is low in most of these areas, bring a bicycle lock, and use it whenever leaving your bicycle out of eyesight. There are many restaurants and parks along the way; don't let the lack of a lock prevent you from exploring them.

Most trails are officially open to the public during daylight hours (dawn to dusk). Come prepared with lights (white for headlights, red for taillights) in the event of poor visibility due to weather or other factors.

On shared-use paths, walkers and cyclists travel on the right side of the trail, with walkers staying to the far right as cyclists pass. Cyclists should announce their passing, usually by ringing a bell and with a friendly statement such as "passing on your left." In some communities, this convention may differ; be sure to defer to local signage. Florida law requires cyclists to obey all traffic controls and signals.

Here's a quick glance at some of Florida's bicycle laws:

- Helmets are required for bicyclists under the age of 16.
- Pedestrians and persons with disabilities have the right-of-way.
- Bicyclists must obey all traffic signals and controls.
- Bicyclists are not permitted to wear headphones, headsets, or other listening devices.
- Lights (front and rear) are required if riding between sunset and sunrise.

For more information, see Florida Statutes 316.2065 and 316.304. Although helmets are not required for adults, they are recommended for all cyclists to help prevent head or brain injury in the event of a collision.

When you choose to undertake a multiday excursion, you must decide if you will carry your own gear or have a support vehicle. This decision profoundly changes the nature of the trip. For me, much of the fun and adventure of multiday bicycle touring comes from being self-sufficient. If you like this idea, too, you will need to figure out how you will carry your extra clothes, necessities, and camping gear (if camping). For walkers, a backpack is the usual solution. For cyclists, there are many options for packing your gear on the bike itself, which is considerably more comfortable than carrying a backpack while riding.

Bicycle saddlebags are often called "panniers," a term derived from the French word for a breadbasket. There are many pannier options, and the prices vary accordingly. Large bike shops often sell them, and a bit of research can help you determine the con-figuration that best suits your needs. Panniers attach to the bikes by different methods, but they usually require a rack. It is a good

Bicycle with waterproof panniers for carrying gear

idea to buy the rack and panniers at the same time to ensure they are compatible. For a short bicycle tour, large seat packs, triangle frame packs, and/or handlebar bags may be sufficient to carry what you need. For me, a crucial requirement is that bags carrying gear are waterproof. If you get caught in the rain, it is reassuring to know that your clothing and gear will still be dry.

Numerous bicycle repair shops are situated along or near the C2C. These shops typically sell bicycle parts and offer repair services, and some rent bicycles. Flat tires are probably the most common bicycle repair issue; unfortunately, they usually don't happen in front of a bike shop. At a minimum, bicyclists should carry a spare tube, tube repair kit, and either a pump or CO_2 cartridges. Another useful repair item is a bicycle-specific multitool (sometimes referred to as an "all-in-one" tool) for adjustments and repairs. And of course, before heading out on a bicycle excursion, be sure your bicycle is in good working condition. If you aren't sure how to do this yourself, visit your local bike shop for a quick tune-up before leaving home.

For long-distance walkers, the most important considerations are shoes and a backpack. The C2C is paved, making hiking boots unnecessary, but good sturdy walking shoes may be in order. As for backpacks, there are many different varieties on the market. Size is the first consideration and depends on how much you plan to carry. To make sure a backpack fits comfortably, try it out with weight inside it. Padding on shoulders and hips straps are important. You will want to carry water and have it easily accessible, so look for water-bottle holders. A good retail outfitter will work to ensure a pack fits your body well. Most importantly, try out your gear (including shoes) before heading out on a long trip.

Long excursions require another logistical consideration: how to get to the beginning of the trail and what to do once you've reached the other end. Obviously, having a good friend or family member who will provide drop-off and pickup services is ideal but not always possible. If traveling with others, you can create your own shuttle service, dropping a vehicle off at the end, then driving together to the start location. Some small groups designate a support vehicle and take turns driving. We've also met individuals whose partners drive and meet them at the end of each day.

Another option, especially if traveling the entire length of the C2C, is to leave a car at the start, then rent a vehicle at the end to drive back. Commercial car rental agencies have locations in both Titusville and St. Petersburg. The volume of trail traffic on some of the longer shared-use trails in the United States has resulted in commercial enterprises that shuttle trail users. As of publication, West Orange Trail Bikes & Blades, a bike shop located at the C2C's Killarney Station trailhead, offers end-to-end shuttle services.

Try to plan lodging accommodations in advance. While Florida has many hotels, sections of the C2C passes through small towns and rural areas with minimal lodging options. Sometimes, a short detour can take you to chain hotels along highways. For example, while the historic area of Sanford has limited lodging, hotels can be found at the intersection of I-4 and First Street, outside of the historic town center and only about a half mile from the C2C. I have provided some suggested itineraries based on daily mileage and lodging availability in the chapter Practical Planning: Suggested Itineraries and Resources.

For the most up-to-date information on lodging in an area, use internet searches and hotel booking websites, such as hotwire.com, kayak.com, expedia.com, booking.com, travelocity.com, or trip advisor.com, or simply search the term "lodging" on Google Maps.

For alternative accommodations, try Airbnb or Warmshowers. **Airbnb** offers stays in places ranging from a single bedroom in a home to the rental of a complete home (https://www.airbnb.com). **Warmshowers** is a nonprofit organization that provides a community network of home-based lodging for traveling cyclists (https://www.warmshowers.org).

If you like to camp, campgrounds are noted within each trail segment chapter and in Practical Planning: Suggested Itineraries and Resources. Contact campgrounds in advance for reservations and availability.

The maps in this book show the route of the C2C, but for the latest information and details, refer to online resources, which have fundamentally changed the travel experience. This is particularly true with regard to GPS location services and resources such as Google Maps. Take advantage of electronic services such as the 100 Florida Trails (www.100floridatrails.com) and Map My Ride (www.mapmyride.com) websites as well as routes posted by other users on programs such as Strava or Ride with GPS. Use a map and compass if you want to travel "old school." I made every effort to identify confusing turns on the trail, and these are included in each trail chapter under the heading "The Route: Need to Know." At the time of publication, much of the trail signage continues to use the original name of the local trail that was built prior to envisioning of the C2C. I have included the regional trail names in each chapter to help in navigation.

For consistency, I use mileage measured one way between two points, including the mileage for the optional spur trails. Remember to double that mileage if you are doing out-and-back trips. For the few instances where walking/hiking trails near the C2C are loop trails, the text indicates this and states mileage for the complete loop.

At the time of publication, there is a 28-mile gap of the C2C Trail between Groveland and the Withlacoochee State Trail, east of Brooksville. Enthusiastic cyclists have found ways to traverse this gap. I address this gap in detail in the Appendix and provide possible options for crossing it. Path construction is already underway on the western end of the gap, but other sections are still in the design phase.

I have made every attempt to provide clear and accurate information about Florida's C2C route. However, the world is dynamic, and change is constant. Alterations in trail conditions and signage and repair or upgrades to facilities will inevitably occur. Detours around construction projects are possible. Use this book in conjunction with other available resources to enhance the success and pleasure of your trail excursions.

FLORIDA'S HERITAGE ALONG THE C2C PATH

Swaying palm trees, sandy beaches, and sunny skies might first spring to mind when you think of Florida, but the state is much more interesting and varied than that. Lush vegetation, wetlands, cypress domes, sandhill and scrub ecosystems, freshwater springs and lakes, and charming small towns are unsung treasures of the Sunshine State. The state also offers a thriving arts culture, culinary delights, and captivating stories of local history. The C2C path invites you to discover a Florida that many tourists never see.

The foundation of the C2C was built by industrious railway businessmen and laborers of the late 1800s. Today's path uses much of the land on which those tracks were laid. But the story of the C2C region also includes the early indigenous people of the area, the first European explorers, the wars fought between settlers and the Seminole Tribe, citrus growers and cattle ranchers, and the beautiful and bountiful natural resources that have lured people to Florida for centuries.

Florida owes its unique shape and land formations to the dynamic nature of geological forces. The relatively flat geography of the Florida peninsula, which makes it wonderful for bicycling, also makes it particularly vulnerable to changes in ocean levels. Over the ages, the land has been repeatedly submerged and reexposed. The peninsula was completely under water, covered by a shallow ocean, for millions of years. During the last Great Ice Age, gigantic glaciers were created from evaporated ocean water, and sea levels fell dramatically. At that time, the peninsula was nearly three times as large as it is now. As glaciers melted at the end of the ice age (nearly 12,000 years ago), sea level rose once again, and the land formation became what we recognize today as Florida.

The earliest known human inhabitants of Florida arrived around the end of that last ice age. The state's subtropical climate provided a hospitable home for early indigenous people. Evidence of these early inhabitants comes in the form of burial mounds and shell middens. Several of these ancient mound sites, such as Windover, Hontoon Island, Safety Harbor, and Weeden Island, are in the central part of the state, although none are directly along the C2C Trail. These early inhabitants lived in Florida alongside mammoths, bison, bears, and saber-tooth cats.

European exploration of the area began in 1513 when Spaniard Juan Ponce de León arrived. De León is credited with giving Florida its name, *La Florida*, in appreciation of its lush vegetation and in honor of the Easter season, during which he landed, known as *Pascua Florida* (the Festival of Flowers). After De León's expedition, further exploration and surveying were done by other Spanish, French, and British explorers; subsequently, control over the land was frequently contested. Colonial rulers changed multiple times until Florida was ceded by Spain to the United States of America in 1821, and the territory was later admitted to the United States as the 27th state in 1845.

The increase of European settlers led to conflicts with the Seminole Tribe, for whom Florida was home. Three wars were conducted in the 1800s by the US army in an attempt to remove native people from Florida (the Seminole Wars are sometimes characterized as one long war, with three major campaigns). These military actions drove the Seminoles into south Florida or relocated them to Oklahoma. As a result, by the 1850s only a few hundred Seminoles remained in secluded areas of southern Florida, and the US government ended its military campaign against them. Seminole County, through which the C2C passes, was named for this native American tribe that the US government fought so hard to eliminate.

After it gained statehood, Florida's population grew rapidly. Agriculture, cattle, and mining businesses thrived. Citrus growing and packing, in particular, became major commercial operations. To meet the demand created by the economic growth of the late 1800s, industrialists looked for reliable means to transport goods, including citrus, and it was during this time that the backbone of the C2C Trail was built, not as a bicycle trail, of course, but as a railroad. Sizeable stretches of today's C2C Trail between the western terminus in St. Petersburg (near the shores of the Gulf of Mexico) to Sanford (on the shores of Lake Monroe) follow the path of a defunct narrow-gauge train route, the Orange Belt Railway. This railway was built in the 1880s and grew primarily through the efforts of Peter Demens. Demens was a Russian-born entrepreneur, builder, and businessman who emigrated to Florida and cofounded the city of St. Petersburg. The Sanford terminus of his Orange Belt Railway was strategic in that it connected the train route with the St. Johns River, a major transportation link for exploration and commerce.

Orange Belt Railway train and the company's president Peter Demens. Photograph taken in Pinellas County, Florida, circa 1888. From the collection of Donald R. Hensley, Jr., www.taplines.net.

Alongside the other economic success stories of the time, the creation of railways coincided with the prosperity of the sponge harvesting industry in Tarpon Springs, a distinctive town along the C2C. Sponges that were harvested from the waters off Tarpon Springs could be readily shipped to far-off markets on the new railways, and the industry's influence on Tarpon Springs endures even today.

The eastern end of the C2C from Titusville to Osteen also owes its existence to an early railroad. The area surrounding Titusville along the Indian River (a 121-mile brackish inland waterway along the east coast) was a very productive citrus growing region. A railroad was built in 1885 to connect Titusville to an inland transportation hub about 35 miles away on the north side of Lake Monroe. From there, the citrus or other goods could be further transported either by steamboats on the St. Johns River or by other railroads leading north to Jacksonville or west to Tampa. The C2C follows much of this railway's original path. The small community of Osteen, which hosts a C2C trailhead, was one of the stations on the original railway.

The regions spanned by the C2C look much different today than they did to the early railway operators. Although some land is preserved in its natural state, the C2C passes through many residential areas and commercial businesses on property that was once undisturbed natural areas or agricultural acreage. By the late 1800s, Orange and Lake Counties had thriving, prosperous citrus groves spreading over miles on undulating countryside. The 226-foot-high Citrus Tower in Clermont was built in 1956 so that visitors could gaze across acres of citrus groves planted on the gently rolling hills. The tower still stands, and you can ride an elevator to the glass-enclosed observation deck on the top. Although some citrus groves still exist here, the view today is dramatically different, as you'll see homes and commercial development instead of agricultural enterprises.

The state's weather, natural beauty, and bountiful resources that once enticed European explorers to its shores now draw vacationers and legions of new residents. Florida's natural environmental lands and wildlife habitats are under continual pressure from suburban and commercial development. Demand for freshwater resources is projected to outstrip supply. Like any area with a growing population, Florida wrestles with issues relating to affordable housing, traffic congestion, pollution, and the destruction of natural habitat. Civic leaders and residents endeavor to balance the conflicting interests.

BUILDING AND CONNECTING THE TRAIL

The early seeds of a C2C path began in 1984 when the Pinellas County Bicycle Advisory Committee recommended that a railroad right-of-way purchased by the Florida Department of Transportation be used to create a bicycle path. This was the beginning of the Pinellas Trail, and its first five-mile section opened in 1990. This original trail (which has since been expanded and improved) became an inspiration and example for other long-distance trail projects in Florida.

Years later, planners and trail enthusiasts envisioned a coast-to-coast path that would take advantage of the growing network of existing trails. The backbone of the C2C includes the East Central Regional Rail Trail, Seminole Wekiva Trail, West Orange Trail, South Lake Trail, Good Neighbor Trail, Suncoast Trail, Tri-County Trail, and Pinellas Trail. The fact that the C2C is a consolidation of numerous separately planned and built trails can sometimes lead to confusion for trail riders, but signage continues to improve as the full length of C2C Trail is fine-tuned and upgraded.

Many governmental entities are involved in the construction and maintenance of the C2C. The Florida Department of Transportation and the Florida Department of Environmental Protection are essential to the process, as are the city and county governments through which the trail passes. The Florida Greenways and Trails System was adopted by the state legislature in 1999 and includes statewide plans and goals regarding land trails for hiking, walking, and bicycling as well as for paddling trails in the lakes, rivers, and coastal waters of the state. See https://florida dep.gov/parks/ogt/content/online-trail-guide.

The popularity of Florida's shared-use trails and the benefits they provide demonstrate how valuable these trails are to residents and visitors alike. While engaging in healthy exercise, trail users explore new towns, enjoy social interactions, and connect to nature. The C2C is a success story for Florida and a bold model for future trails.

TRAIL SECTION 1
TITUSVILLE TO OSTEEN

BREVARD AND VOLUSIA COUNTIES, INCLUDING TITUSVILLE, MAYTOWN, AND OSTEEN. OPTIONAL SPUR TRAIL TO NEW SMYRNA BEACH

Trail section length: 30 miles
Point A: Titusville Welcome Center, 419 S. Hopkins Ave.
Point B: Osteen Civic Center trailhead, 165 New Smyrna Blvd.
20-mile optional spur trail to New Smyrna Beach

HIGHLIGHTS
Titusville's small, historic town center
Aerospace industry and history
Black Point Wildlife Drive, Merritt Island
Cycling through rural, natural lands

TRAILHEADS
Parrish Park, 1 A. Max Brewer Memorial Parkway, Titusville
Titusville Welcome Center, 419 South Hopkins Ave., Titusville
Chain of Lakes Park, 2300 Truman Scarborough Way, Titusville
Maytown Spur Trailhead, Maytown Spur Road, Oak Hill
Gobbler's Lodge Trailhead, Gobbler's Lodge Road, Osteen
Osteen Civic Center, 165 New Smyrna Blvd., Osteen

Trail Section 1 – Titusville to Osteen

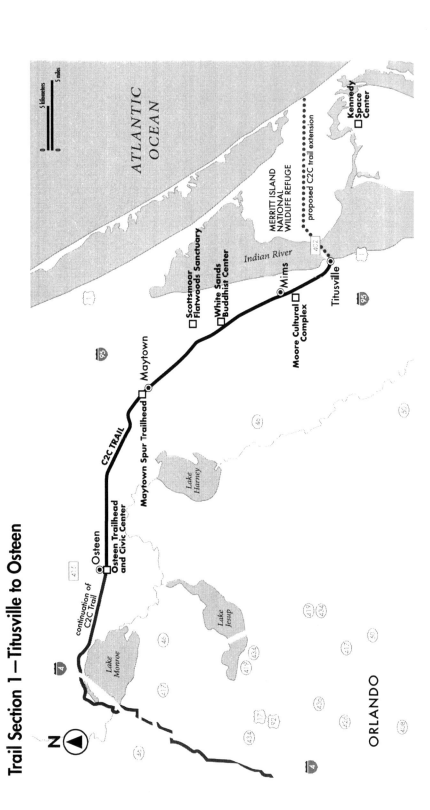

THE ROUTE: NEED TO KNOW

This section of the C2C path follows the East Central Regional Rail Trail in Brevard and Volusia Counties. Much of the trail is remote, with miles of peaceful cycling and opportunities to see wildlife. Bring plenty of water and sunscreen because there are few facilities available. The trail is well marked, with few intersections.

The official beginning/end of the C2C path is currently in the center of **Titusville**. The **Titusville Welcome Center** has maps, water, restrooms, and a small bicycle shop. The dedicated shared-use C2C path starts at 204 Canaveral Ave., one block north of Main Street, which is less than half a mile of easy cycling from the Welcome Center.

At the time of publication, the 10-mile route from Parrish Park eastward to Playalinda Beach is still in the development stage. When complete, this trail extension will provide bicycling access to stunning, unspoiled Atlantic Ocean beaches.

The 17 miles between Titusville and Maytown are flat and easy to ride, particularly because the route is straightforward and without many intersections. Be aware that there are no water fountains or restrooms and few commercial facilities.

In Maytown, near the intersection of Maytown Road and Maytown Spur Road, two paved shared-use paths intersect. At this intersection, the main C2C path follows a NW/SE direction. The second path, a 90-degree turn off the C2C, heads northeast to Edgewater and on to New Smyrna Beach as part of the St. John's River-to-Sea Loop (see "Optional Spur Trail to New Smyrna Beach" below).

Hotel lodging in this section is scarce except for the Titusville area. In the center of Titusville, there are a small number of motels and B&B accommodations. Several chain hotels are situated near the intersection of I-4 and SR 50, about seven miles from the C2C, southwest of the historic downtown area.

At the western end of this segment is the small **Osteen Civic Center**. The Civic Center building is generally not open to the public, but the trailhead has public restrooms, car parking, tables, and benches.

Downtown Titusville

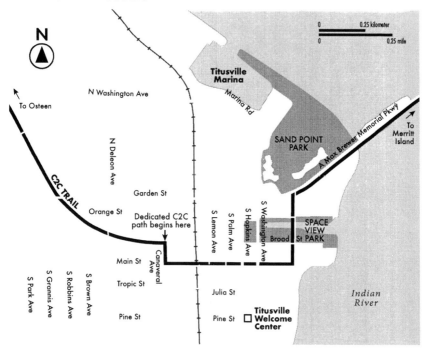

RECOMMENDED WALKS

Walk across the **A. Max Brewer Bridge** from Titusville's **Space View Park** to **Parrish Park** and you will not be alone; this is a popular exercise routine for locals. Along the way, you will enjoy refreshing sea breezes and panoramic views of the Indian River, including boats, birds, and even bottlenose dolphins. The walk between Space View Park on the mainland and Parrish Park on Merritt Island is just over one mile. At Parrish Park, enjoy watching the activity of the seabirds and fishermen. The bridge is designed with pedestrians in mind: a concrete barrier separates the sidewalk from motor traffic.

For a short hike between two pleasing destinations, trek the three miles of the paved C2C Trail between **downtown Titusville** to **Chain of Lakes Park** (2300 Truman Scarborough Way, Titusville). At the southern end of this walk in Titusville, you can enjoy a drink, quiet meal, or snack. At **Chain of Lakes Park**, relax at the picnic pavilions or the playground. Restrooms and water fountains are also located here.

Within **Chain of Lakes Park** there are more than three miles of nature trails, including a 50-foot-tall wildlife viewing tower. To reach the park from the C2C, head east at the intersection of Dairy Road (there is a wide sidewalk/path along Dairy Road). The entrance to the park is just 0.3 mile from the C2C. For more information about this park, see "Nature" below.

For a stroll with a historical perspective, meander through the streets of **Downtown Titusville**, particularly along Washington Avenue and Indian River Avenue, between Orange Street to the north and South Street to the south. Twenty-four buildings in this area are on the National Register of Historic Places, including the Queen Anne architectural style **Pritchard House** (424 South Washington Ave.), which is open to the public. This compact town center includes a variety of small restaurants and shops. Be sure to visit **Space View Park** (17 Orange St.), which honors the men and women of the US space exploration program.

For a **remote walk** along the C2C, start at the **Maytown Spur Trailhead**. Heading southeast from here, the paved path immediately ventures into a quiet, isolated area. The trail is straight and without elevation gain, but its real allure is the opportunity to relish peaceful nature and to see wildlife, particularly at dawn and dusk. Make this out-and-back walk as long or short as you want to venture. Seven miles southeast from the Maytown Spur trailhead is the first sign of civilization where busy I-95 crosses over the path; the White Sands Buddhist Center is just 0.25 mile farther south. There are no facilities along this remote path.

Much of the C2C path between Titusville and Osteen is unshaded and has few facilities. Walkers undertaking this section should be sure to bring plenty of water, snacks, and sunscreen.

LOCAL CULTURE

Titusville is a small, relatively quiet town that has both humble charm and an interesting history. Part of the appeal of Titusville is its laid-back style and an atmosphere of being in "old Florida." The city is perhaps best known today for its role in the US space exploration program but has long served as a gateway to extraordinary wildlife-viewing opportunities, most notably the Merritt Island National Wildlife Refuge (see "Nature" below). Tourism is currently a major local economic driver; in addition to rocket launches and wildlife viewing, visitors come to Titusville for its good weather and the beautiful beaches nearby. More recently, its downtown core has seen increased activity and revitalized local businesses, partly due to trail users.

Downtown Titusville includes the **C2C Welcome Center** and bicycle shop (419 S. Hopkins Ave.), small stores, a bakery, breweries, and restaurants. The city marina is located less than a mile north of the Welcome Center, adjacent to **Sand Point Park**.

To get a glimpse of Titusville's role in the space program, head to **Space View Park** (8 Broad St. or access from Orange St.). There, you can wander among the outdoor memorials and monuments dedicated to America's space exploration and the astronauts and workers essential to the program. The **American Space Museum** (308 Pine St.) tells the story of space exploration through exhibits, including a wide range of artifacts such as astronaut suits, launch consoles, and memorabilia donated by NASA employees.

If you're lucky enough to be in town when a **rocket launch** is scheduled, one of the best places in the town center for a good view is a city-owned piece of land at the intersection of Main Street and Indian River Avenue. Kennedy Space Center's launchpads are directly east from this property. Locals will congregate here, too, but it's generally not too crowded because anyplace along the water will afford a view of a rising rocket. The C2C overpass at Garden Street is another fun spot for rocket viewing. For launch schedules, use the Kennedy Space Center Events Calendar online.

Space Shuttle Monument at Titusville's Space View Park

For a fee, visitors can tour the impressive **Kennedy Space Center** on Merritt Island (https://www.kennedyspacecenter .com/) (13 miles from the Titusville Welcome Center, not easily accessible by bicycle). The visitor complex has a wide range of interactive exhibits, an actual lunar landing module, enormous Saturn V rockets, a Shuttle Launch Experience, and much more.

Although this book is not a restaurant guide, a discussion of Titusville would not be complete without mentioning **Dixie**

Crossroads (1475 Garden St.). This iconic restaurant serves generous portions of seafood and southern specialties in a casual and lively atmosphere.

Along the C2C, be sure to visit the beautiful and peaceful **White Sands Buddhist Center** (4640 Knost Dr., Mims). The Center is about six miles north of Mims, just south of the intersection of the C2C and I-95. Keep a close lookout for a small sign on the trail directing you to a narrow path; it can be easy to miss due

A 35-foot-tall statue of Buddha serenely greets visitors at the White Sands Buddhist Center.

to dense vegetation. The Center offers a tranquil place of meditation and natural beauty. Meditation services are held each Sunday morning in both English and Vietnamese. Visitors are welcome to quietly experience the Center and wander through its gardens among the beautiful enormous sculptures and carved works of art transported from Asia. The three largest granite statues of Buddha in Florida are located on this property. The location was carefully chosen for its secluded tranquility.

The **region west of Mims** prides itself on its rural setting and agricultural economy. Farmton, halfway between the Maytown Spur trailhead and Osteen, is an unincorporated area of Volusia County, and although noted on maps, there is no town center. A huge swath of land called the Farmton Tract is owned by the Miami Corporation (formerly International Harvester), a large private corporation that uses land resources in this area primarily for agriculture, ranching, and the growing of trees for harvesting (silviculture). The area is managed in cooperation with governmental agencies and according to long-term plans designed to conserve important wetlands, wildlife corridors, and habitats.

NATURE

For nature lovers, the eastern portion of the C2C is a delight. Immediately east of Titusville is the **Merritt Island National Wildlife Refuge** and the renowned **Black Point Wildlife Drive**, a wintertime mecca for birders and wildlife enthusiasts. This refuge is a by-product of the security and safety buffers put in place for the space program, thus preserving acres of pristine natural land. The area is home to a wide variety of species, including alligators, manatees, and bobcats and a large variety of native and migratory birds, including Osprey, Bald Eagles, Great Egrets, Belted Kingfishers, and Roseate Spoonbills.[2] In addition, endangered animals,

---

2. I use title case capitalization of common bird names per the 2014 adoption of this convention by the American Ornithologist Union. This clarifies the distinction between a description of, for example, a yellow warbler, and the species of bird named the Yellow Warbler.

such as the Florida Scrub Jay, make their home in the Refuge's scrub habitat.

To get to Merritt Island from Titusville by bicycle, cross the Indian River on the A. Max Brewer Memorial Causeway. A planned extension of the C2C route will eventually cross Merritt Island and continue out to the Atlantic Ocean beaches. Roads in this area are sometimes restricted due to rocket launches or NASA work hours. Currently, there is no road shoulder or bike path east of Parrish Park.

Black Point Wildlife Drive, a one-way seven-mile drive, is ideal for wildlife viewing. Although most visitors tour the wildlife drive in cars (the speed limit is 15 mph), the unpaved road is suitable for bicycles. Wide touring, gravel, or mountain bike tires are most comfortable on this surface. Entrance to the wildlife drive is three miles northeast of the A. Max Brewer Causeway Bridge.

The **Merritt Island NWR Visitor Center** (1987 Scrub Jay Way, Titusville) has interesting exhibits, educational displays, and a gift shop as well as restrooms and water fountains. Directly outside the Visitor Center is a pleasant pond and a shaded walking path. The Visitor Center is an excellent gateway to exploring this outstanding natural area. Note that access to the Refuge may be limited when a rocket launch is scheduled. The Visitor Center is four miles east of the A. Max Brewer Causeway Bridge.

A **manatee** observation deck is located on SR 3 on the east side of the Haulover Canal Bridge (spring and fall are the best seasons for manatee viewing here, but they have been spotted year-round). This observation deck is approximately 12 miles from downtown Titusville. Currently, there is no dedicated bicycle trail to this site. If you are lucky enough to see a manatee, you will be amazed by these huge, slow, gentle creatures. These herbivores live in both fresh and salt water, but they struggle to thrive due to loss of habitat, collisions with boats, food scarcity, and water pollution.

For those who want to get out on the water, outfitters offer **kayaking and paddleboard tours** of the Indian River and

Windover Archeological Site

Titusville's prime location, close to the ocean but protected from it, and just east of the St. Johns River, provided an ideal spot for ancient populations. Five miles south of Titusville is the Windover Archeological Site. Although this site is not suitable for visiting (it is in a swamp with no trail access), it is considered one of the most important archeological finds in the United States. While building a road in 1982, construction workers discovered a muck pond containing human bones. Work was halted and archeologists brought in. The subsequent analysis of the area found well-preserved skeletal remains of over 160 individuals who lived in the Middle Archaic period (5,000–6,000 BC). The burial practice of placing bodies in peat and water helped preserve the remains over the millennia. This important archeological discovery reveals much about how these people lived. Woven textiles, projectiles, shells, animal bones, and storage containers from the site provide detailed information about these early inhabitants of Florida.

The Florida State University Digital Library provides access to detailed field notes and photographs from the site. See https://fsu.digital.flvc.org/islandora/object/fsu:windover.

Mosquito Lagoon. Paddlers can experience the amazing sight of **bioluminescent plankton** during evening trips. These organisms emit light in an eerie display in response to movement, such as fish swimming by or your paddle and boat moving through the water. For a peak bioluminescence experience, paddle in summer or fall when the water is warm and the phase of the moon guarantees a dark sky.

Along the C2C, three miles north of Titusville, is **Chain of Lakes Park** (2300 Truman Scarborough Way). You can easily

An honor-system rest stop for cyclists near Maytown

access the park from the C2C via a 0.3-mile paved path/wide sidewalk on Truman Scarborough Way. The park was created as a watershed management project, designed to help protect the Indian River Lagoon by trapping and filtering polluted stormwater. The result of this endeavor is a 92-acre park of beautiful artificial wetlands and lakes that now provide excellent habitat for plants and animals. Limpkins, herons, egrets, ducks, hawks, warblers, woodpeckers, and even Bald Eagles can be seen here. Chain of Lakes Park is part of the Great Florida Birding Trail, and over 170 species of birds have been spotted at this location.

The quiet and isolated 26 miles between Mims and Osteen are a welcome escape from the hectic world. Here, you will experience an excellent example of Florida's **flatwoods ecosystems**. In Florida, flatwoods usually contain a mixture of pine forests, marshes, swamps, and cypress wetlands. The system's health is reliant on periodic fires and natural intermittent flooding. Although Florida lacks significant elevation changes, just a few inches can dramatically change an ecosystem. Look for drier, sandy areas as well as natural wet depressions and notice the difference in vegetation. Florida environments that experience fluctuations in freshwater levels can support iconic southeastern trees, such as swamp tupelo and cypress, both of which can be seen along the trail.

When crossing over creeks, stop on the small bridges to look for alligators and wading birds. Because some stretches of the trail are remote, there have been reports of bobcats (which are relatively small, skittish, and likely to run away if they see you). Also, look for Gray Catbirds, Swallow-tailed Kites, White Ibises, Wild Turkey, and Northern Cardinals. The forested sections closer to Osteen are home to many woodpeckers, hawks, and owls.

In this section, the trail crosses through low-lying areas east of **St. Johns River**. The flood-prone nature of this land protected it from rampant development seen elsewhere in the state. You won't see the formidable St. Johns River here, but you will get good views

A recumbent bicyclist enjoys a morning on the trail east of Osteen.

in Trail Section 2 when the C2C crosses it west of Lake Monroe. At over 300 miles, the St. Johns River is Florida's longest river, flowing northward from its marshy headwaters in Indian River County toward Jacksonville and its outlet at the Atlantic Ocean. This river was an important transportation route for early Florida explorers and settlers.

HISTORICAL NOTES

Titusville's namesake was Colonel Henry T. Titus, although the title "colonel" was merely an honorific for this soldier of fortune and not an actual military rank. An entrepreneur, he moved to the area in the mid-1800s and opened several businesses, taking advantage of Titusville's location on the Indian River. The Indian River is part of the intracoastal waterway and provided excellent transportation and shipping opportunities. Colonel Titus built the **Titus House**, a grand hotel adjacent to a saloon, to cater to tourists from as far away as Europe. The hotel, which once stood on Washington Avenue, was unfortunately destroyed by fire in 1964, and only a historical marker remains.

Titusville's growth was stimulated by the Florida land boom of the 1920s and the inception and growth of the US space program in the 1950s, but it was the space race of the 1960s and the Apollo Program that really put Titusville on the map. The Space Shuttle missions that ran from 1981 to 2011 were a boost to Titusville's economy through employment opportunities and the space tourism that followed. The recently reenergized space program of NASA as well as the private sector launches by SpaceX and Blue Origin keep Titusville in the public eye.

This tranquil area was not immune to the hostilities of the civil rights era. Stop at the **Harry T. and Harriet V. Moore Cultural Complex** (2180 Freedom Ave., Mims) to learn about the Moores and their work as early civil rights activists and their tragic deaths (see box below). A replica of the Moores' home, a heritage walking trail, and a park commemorate their lives and promote awareness of the African American experience.

Harry T. and Harriet V. Moore Cultural Complex

Harry and Harriet Moore, leading civil rights activists of the 1930s and 1940s, were murdered when a bomb placed under their home exploded on December 25, 1951. Harry died almost immediately; Harriet died nine days later. No one was ever arrested or held accountable for their murder although FBI investigations suspected members of the Ku Klux Klan.

The Moores organized the first Brevard County chapter for the NAACP (National Advancement of Colored People) in 1934. Harry's work with the Florida Progressive Voter's League was instrumental in registering over 100,000 Black voters in Florida. Both Harry and Harriet were public school teachers in the segregated school system of Brevard County. Both were fired from their jobs in 1945 because of their civil rights efforts and their work toward equal pay for Black public schoolteachers. In 2021, the Brevard County School Board formally acknowledged the injustice of their firing and declared the Moores "Brevard County School Teachers Emeritus" and recognized their outstanding service and significant contributions to the school system, the State of Florida, and the nation.

OPTIONAL SPUR TRAIL TO NEW SMYRNA BEACH

This is a 20-mile spur ride to New Smyrna Beach: 17-mile trail to Edgewater, plus an additional 2.5 miles on road to New Smyrna Beach's Canal Street district.

Take this spur trail to reach the interesting and lively town of New Smyrna Beach. The spur departs from the C2C in Maytown and heads north to the town of Edgewater. Travel 2.5 miles farther on roads to the picturesque downtown of New Smyrna

Spur Trail to New Smyrna Beach

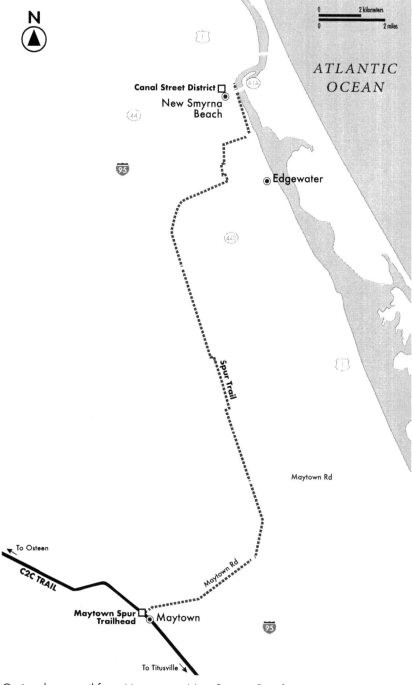

Optional spur trail from Maytown to New Smyrna Beach

Beach. Another three miles to the east of this downtown is the actual beach, replete with beautiful sandy beaches and the chance to swim in the Atlantic Ocean at public beaches.

The dedicated trail currently ends in Edgewater on 10th Street. To get to New Smyrna Beach, turn right (east) on 10th Street and travel 0.75 mile. Cross US 1 at the crosswalk, then continue straight ahead (east) on the cut-through sidewalk. In 200 feet, turn left on Magnolia Street, then immediately right onto 10th Street. At the end of 10th Street, turn left (north) onto scenic Riverside Drive. Follow Riverside Drive 1.5 miles to Canal Street to reach New Smyrna Beach's mainland town center.

New Smyrna Beach is a delightful place to stay overnight during a bicycle or walking tour. Tree-lined **Canal Street**, the small but interesting heart of mainland New Smyrna Beach, is lined with unique shops, breweries, galleries, and restaurants.

Cycle or walk along South Riverside Drive for lovely views of the Indian River as you pass by distinctive waterfront homes. This area of New Smyrna Beach also offers some unique bed-and-breakfast lodging.

For a pleasant place to watch the activity along the Intracoastal Waterway/Indian River, head to **Riverside Park** (299 S. Riverside Dr.) at the east end of Canal Street. This eight-acre park also has a playground, restrooms, gazebo, walking paths, and fishing pier.

Old Fort Park (115 Julia St.) has a misleading name. The coquina ruins on this site appear to be an old Spanish fort, but its origins are a mystery. Some historians speculate that the ruins are not a fort at all but perhaps the remnants of a mansion or a church. Coquina is a sedimentary limestone rock primarily composed of broken seashells. It is formed when seashells accumulate on the shore over hundreds of years, then are submerged and solidified over long periods of time. In a locale such as Florida, which lacks strong rock such as granite, slate, or quartz, coquina became a valuable building material for the Spanish settlers. One of the notable examples of a surviving coquina structure is the beautiful Castillo de San Marcos, a fort in St. Augustine, Florida.

The **New Smyrna Beach Museum of History** (120 Sams Ave.) hosts exhibits on local history and archeology but, more notably, also houses the unique **East Coast Surfing Museum**. The display uses surfboards, surfing memorabilia, art, and historic photographs to tell the story of the surfing community of the area.

The beachside area of the town of New Smyrna Beach can be somewhat congested due to the sprawl of homes and condominiums, but there are plenty of good seafood restaurants and shops in addition to the allure of the beaches themselves. **Flagler Avenue** is fun for its beach-infused character of its eateries and retail stores, including surf shops.

Flagler Avenue Beachfront Park (201 Buenos Aires St.) is an excellent spot to access the sandy beach and has public restrooms. To reach Flagler Avenue Beachfront Park by bicycle, cross the Indian River on either the Highway A1A South Causeway or North Causeway. Both have wide shoulders and/or sidewalks that can be used by cyclists. If you use the A1A South Causeway, turn north after crossing the Indian River for approximately one mile until you reach Flagler Avenue. If using the North Causeway, stay on the causeway across the Indian River, after which the causeway becomes Flagler Avenue. It is just over two miles between mainland Riverside Park and the beachside Flagler Avenue Beachfront Park.

The **Marine Discovery Center** (520 Barracuda Blvd.) provides a unique look into Florida's fragile coastal ecosystems, specifically the salt marshes and mangroves of the Indian River Lagoon. The Center is 0.3 mile from the intersection of Barracuda Boulevard and North Causeway. The Center's mission is to protect and restore coastal ecosystems, and it focuses on hands-on community engagement to promote its goals. There is a small educational display area at the Center, but more intriguing are efforts to engage the public through educational programs, volunteer opportunities, pontoon boat tours, and kayak expeditions in the Indian River Lagoon. For more information and schedules of boat tours and other activities, contact the Center at https://www.marinediscoverycenter.org.

Although this spur is not part of the official route of the C2C, it provides an opportunity to explore Florida's beautiful east coast beaches and an interesting, vibrant beachside community. The route between Maytown and New Smyrna Beach is part of the planned and partially constructed St. Johns River-to-Sea bicycle loop (https://river2sealoop.org/home).

TRAIL SECTION 2
OSTEEN TO SANFORD

VOLUSIA AND SEMINOLE COUNTIES, INCLUDING THE TOWNS OF OSTEEN AND DEBARY. OPTIONAL SPUR ON THE SPRING-TO-SPRING TRAIL

Trail section length: 13 miles

Point A: Osteen Civic Center Trailhead, 165 New Smyrna Blvd., Osteen

Point B: Lake Monroe Wayside Park, 4150 US 17, Sanford (4.5 miles west of downtown)

2.5-mile optional spur to Beck Ranch Park

24-mile optional spur to DeLeon Springs via the Spring-to-Spring Trail

For details about downtown Sanford and the Sanford Spur Trail, see Trail Section 3.

HIGHLIGHTS
Natural and scenic countryside
Historic Beck Ranch Park
Gemini Springs Park

Trail Section 2—Osteen to Sanford

N

0 1 kilometer
0 1 mile

continuation of C2C

Osteen
Civic Center

Spur Trail to
Beck Ranch Park

BECK
RANCH
PARK

LAKE MONROE
CONSERVATION
AREA

4145

4162

C2C TRAIL

4146

4155

LAKE MONROE
CONSERVATION
AREA

415

GREEN
SPRINGS
PARK

Enterprise

Lake Monroe

Sanford

DeBary
Hall and
Trailhead

4

17
92

GEMINI
SPRINGS
PARK

Spur Trail

17 92 46

To DeLeon
Springs

Spring-to-Spring Trail

continuation
of C2C

LAKE MONROE
WAYSIDE PARK

4

46

TRAILHEADS

Osteen Civic Center Trailhead, 165 New Smyrna Blvd., Osteen
Beck Ranch Park, 751 SR 415, Osteen (2.5 miles south of the
  C2C)
Green Springs Park, 994 Enterprise Osteen Road, Deltona
DeBary Hall Trailhead, 198 Sunrise Blvd., DeBary
Gemini Springs North Trailhead, 30 Dirksen Dr., DeBary
Gemini Springs Park, 37 Dirksen Dr., DeBary
Lake Monroe Park, 975 S. Charles Richard Beall Blvd., DeBary
Lake Monroe Wayside Park, 4150 US 17, Sanford

THE ROUTE: NEED TO KNOW

Along the 13 miles between Osteen and Sanford, you'll travel on
the north side of Lake Monroe and pass through natural, rural,
and residential areas of southern Volusia County. Between Osteen
and Green Springs Park, much of the C2C is on shaded paths. The
trail portion along DeBary Avenue and Dirksen Drive is adjacent
to the road and less protected from sun and traffic noise. The trail
then passes through beautiful scenery in Gemini Springs Park (see
map).

There are several trailheads in this section, but it is important
to carry plenty of water, snacks, and sunscreen because there are
few commercial facilities.

Much of this segment follows the East Central Regional
Rail Trail from Osteen to its termination point at Green Springs.
Heading west from Green Springs, the name of the trail changes
to the Spring-to-Spring Trail.

To cross the St. Johns River at the west edge of Lake Monroe,
C2C users travel between the southern terminus of the Spring-to-
Spring Trail in Gemini Springs Park and Seminole County's trail
system beginning at the western edge of Sanford. This bridge is
the only option to cross the St. Johns River in this vicinity, but the
shared-use path is wide and protected by a concrete barrier from
motorized traffic.

Gemini Springs Area

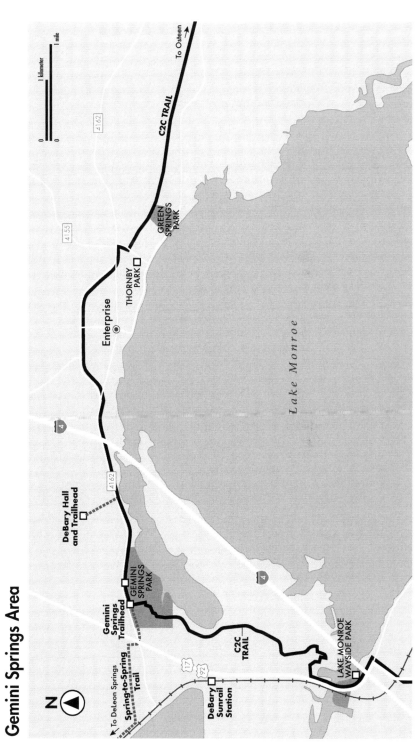

The C2C route near Gemini Springs Park

Hotel lodging in this segment is scarce except where the C2C passes under I-4 in DeBary/Deltona (about 1.5 miles east of Gemini Springs). Camping is available in Gemini Springs Park (37 Dirksen Dr., DeBary) and Lake Monroe Park (975 S. Charles Richard Beall Blvd., DeBary).

RECOMMENDED WALKS

Several scenic walks can be found in this trail segment. Green Springs Park, Gemini Springs Park, and their surrounding areas are ideal for exploring on foot and are good starting points for lengthier walks.

Green Springs Park is a relatively small park of 31 acres, but the pretty sulfur springs and the lush greenery make for a lovely one-mile walk within the park (see "Nature" section below for more information). To add mileage from Green Springs Park, head west on the C2C for 0.5 mile, turn left (south) on the spur trail that runs parallel to Providence Boulevard for 0.1 mile. On the right is **Thornby Park** (110 Providence Blvd., Deltona), which has picnic and restroom facilities and is known for its sizeable playground. This lovely 40-acre property became a park in 2011 after years of effort by local preservationists to save the land from development. Thornby Park has a delightfully verdant 0.5-mile hike.

Gemini Springs Park is a picturesque park for walking or hiking. Some of the designated walks in the park use the paved C2C Trail, while others meander on unpaved loops. A 0.75-mile loop nature trail starts near the east parking lot and can be lengthened by crossing a short bridge to the western side of the park. If you combine all the trails in the park, including the C2C/Spring-to-Spring trail, a total of 4.5 miles of hiking paths can be explored. See "Nature" section below for details about this appealing park.

For a longer hike, travel on the C2C between **Green Springs Park** and the **Osteen Civic Center**. This pleasant 5.5-mile section takes you through quiet environments, crossing just a few lightly traveled roads. Facilities are scarce, but the tranquil nature of the walk makes it an enjoyable one.

Intrepid hikers can cover 7.2 miles on the C2C between **Green Springs Park** and **Lake Monroe Wayside Park**. Over half of this trek is in wooded areas, while the portion of the path adjacent to DeBary Avenue and Dirksen Drive is unsheltered from sun and traffic noise. This walk takes you through Gemini Springs Park and across the St. Johns River Bridge, which affords broad views of the waterway.

LOCAL CULTURE

For a look at the life and times of early Florida ranchers, visit **Beck Ranch Park** (751 SR 415, Osteen), 2.5 miles south of the Osteen Civic Center trailhead. To get there, use the trail parallel to SR 415 (on the southeast side of the road). From the Osteen Civic Center, a one-mile stretch of quiet residential road leads to the SR 415 Trail: travel south on New Smyrna Boulevard, east on Railroad Avenue, south onto Carpenter Drive, and west onto Longwood Drive to SR 415.

Bucolic **Beck Ranch Park** is on 25 acres of land that was once part of a thriving cattle ranch (see "Historical Notes" below for more about Florida's early ranchers). Live Oak trees adorned with Spanish Moss gracefully spread their canopy throughout the park and provide abundant shade. In addition to learning about the history of the area and exploring old buildings such as a corn silo and cattle-weighing pens, you can enjoy shaded picnic pavilions, restrooms, playgrounds, and sports fields, all in a beautiful setting. The park opened in 2014 with funding from Volusia County's land preservation program, Volusia Forever. Beck Ranch Park also serves as a trailhead for hikes into the Lake Monroe Conservation Area, including a two-mile trail through open pasture down to the St. Johns River (four miles out and back).

A short half-mile spur path in DeBary will take you along quiet Mansion Boulevard to **Historic DeBary Hall** (198 Sunrise Blvd). On the C2C, look for the crosswalk at the intersection of Dirksen Drive and Mansion Boulevard to find this spur trail. DeBary Hall is an 8,000-square-foot Victorian home built in 1871 as a hunting

Majestic oak trees create a peaceful place to stop at Beck Ranch Park.

lodge for Frederick deBary, a champagne importer and entrepreneur originally from Germany. DeBary hosted many prominent guests at this winter retreat and later added over 10,000 acres of land to his holdings, on which he planted citrus groves. The historic hall is open to the public. Inside are exhibits, some rooms with period décor, a theater, and a gift shop. You can also explore the mansion's grounds and stables.

The modern-day community of DeBary does not have a true downtown center. However, the city has the important advantage of a **SunRail station** (630 S. Charles Richard Beall Blvd.). SunRail is the region's north-south light rail system, which travels from DeBary southward to Sanford, Winter Park, Orlando, Kissimmee, and Poinciana. This convenience provides opportunities and connections to the C2C for both residents and visitors. Locals can take SunRail to DeBary for easy access to the C2C. Visitors can hop on the train in DeBary to explore other cities and towns.

Florida's Birds

You'll undoubtably see and hear many of Florida's birds while traveling on the C2C. Bird watchers flock to the state, especially in the winter, to enjoy these beautiful creatures. The subtropical climate and plentiful lakes, rivers, and coastal marshes of Florida provide habitat for many interesting species, including wading birds, birds of prey, and migratory warblers. The state bird of Florida is the Mockingbird, which is quite common. Listen for its beautiful and varied calls.

Florida is home to over 1,500 nesting pairs of Bald Eagles. While many spend their summers elsewhere, eagles are regularly seen in Central Florida in fall, winter, and spring. Mated pairs often return to their same nesting spot year after year. Other common birds of prey include Osprey, Red-shouldered Hawks, Swallow-tailed Kites, and Barred Owls. On the coast, you may be treated to Magnificent Frigatebirds, Black Skimmers, pelicans, and terns. If you see a large pink bird, look closely: it is more likely to be a Roseate Spoonbill than a Flamingo.

A Snowy Egret on the hunt for a fish dinner

The DeBary SunRail station is one mile from Gemini Springs Park and is accessible to cyclists and walkers by sidewalks and bike lanes. At the time of publication, SunRail operates primarily as a commuter rail service with operations on weekdays only. See https://sunrail.com for schedules. Bicycles are permitted on the trains with no extra charge.

NATURE

This route segment offers easy access to natural environments including wooded paths, Green Springs Park, Gemini Springs Park, and views of Lake Monroe.

Green Springs Park (994 Enterprise Osteen Rd., Deltona) is a 30-plus-acre park with an unusual and slightly eerie green sulfur spring (no swimming permitted). The spring is in a beautiful setting amid lush vegetation. There is a well-signed, dedicated path entrance from the C2C in addition to the main entrance on Enterprise Osteen Road. Indigenous people believed that the sulfur content of the spring water had healing powers. The vegetative ecosystem is robust, and the Florida Native Plant Society identified nearly 100 different plant species on this property. Ferns love the dense shade of the park, and eight distinct fern species were observed. The unique spring is easy to find once you enter the park; look for signs from the parking lot. Restrooms and benches are available.

For a view of **Lake Monroe**, head to Green Springs Park's main entrance on the southwest side of the park. The nearby **Lake Monroe Boat Ramp** (966 Lakeshore Dr., Deltona) is a public boat ramp with expansive views and provides local boaters and fishermen with prime access to the lake. To get there, exit from Green Springs Park's main entrance, and turn right (west). The road's name immediately changes from Enterprise Osteen Road to Lakeshore Drive. The public boat ramp is approximately 500 feet from Green Springs Park's main entrance.

Lake Monroe is a massive 15-square-mile lake that is part of the **St. Johns River** system. The St. Johns River is known as a "river of lakes" because of the numerous lakes it strings together during its 300-mile journey to the sea. This natural river/lake combination is partially due to the mere 30-foot elevation change over the river's length. Lake Monroe is considered a superb fishing spot of the region. Anglers ply these waters for largemouth bass, striped bass, black crappie, bluegill, and sunfish. Sailboats can often be seen out in Lake Monroe, and weekly races are hosted by the Lake Monroe Sailing Association based in Sanford.

On the northwest corner of Lake Monroe, the C2C passes through noteworthy **Gemini Springs Park** (37 Dirksen Dr., DeBary). This park preserves over 200 acres of natural beauty and offers many recreational opportunities.

Gemini Springs Park is home to two of Florida's many **freshwater springs** (the presence of two springs here gives the park its name). Spring water flows out of the underground aquifer, bubbling up to the surface at a constant 72° F temperature year-round. At Gemini Springs, you can get a close look at this marvel;

The trail through Gemini Springs Park invites visitors to slow down and appreciate Florida's natural environment.

45

Cypress Trees

While cycling and hiking through low-lying areas of Central Florida you will certainly see cypress trees with their distinctive "knees" protruding around the base of trunks. Two types of cypress trees are native to Florida: Bald Cypress (*Taxodium distichum*) and Pond Cypress (*Taxodium ascendens*). Look for them in wetlands and swamps. Cypress trees can grow for hundreds of years and may reach over 150 feet tall. In the autumn, the leaves turn a beautiful rusty orange color before falling off.

The exact purpose of their woody knees is unknown, though many scientists speculate that they provide the tree structural stability. The knees are most often found with trees that grow in flood-prone areas or in swamps.

Cypress swamps can be uncommonly beautiful. Stop to enjoy a stand of cypress trees in dark water. Note their strikingly thin leaves, unusual bark, and odd knees, and savor the serene and primeval atmosphere. Cypress swamps provide an extraordinary environment for a multitude of plants and animals including wading birds, epiphytes (air plants), ferns, river otters, and alligators.

a boardwalk next to the springs offers excellent views. In addition to their importance to the natural ecosystem, the underground aquifer is the main source of drinking water for Central and North Florida. To find the springs, you'll need to turn off the paved trail onto a hiking path; it is less than a quarter mile away from the C2C/Spring-to-Spring trail path.

For a look at another unusual geological feature of Florida, walk a short distance north of the springs to see a fenced-off **sinkhole**. This sinkhole opened in 2017 and is an example of a dramatic "cover-collapse" event. The roof of an underground cavern collapsed, possibly relating to heavy rainfall, and the collapse exposed the cavern underneath. Often, the underground cavern is much larger than the visible hole at the surface.

Gemini Springs Park is a beautiful place, worthy of stopping for the scenery, a short hike, a picnic, or even overnight camping. The setting is picturesque and offers access to both nature and recreational activities.

HISTORICAL NOTES

The community of **Osteen** was named for a 19th-century cattle rancher, Hezekiah Osteen, who had settled and worked in this area. For insight into the lives of Florida's cattle ranchers of the past, visit **Beck Ranch Park** (751 SR 415, Osteen, 2.5 miles south of the C2C). The cattle of this region were reportedly hardy animals, descendants of cattle brought to Florida by Spanish explorers and settlers.

A customized bicycle rack at Beck Ranch pays tribute to the cattle that roamed here.

Prior to the development of dedicated ranches, Florida cattle were left to roam and graze on open land. Cowboys would round up and herd the cattle to designated ports in Southwest Florida, where they would be sold to dealers. For a captivating tale that portrays this time period, I recommend Patrick D. Smith's novel, *A Land Remembered.* The novel tells the story of three generations of Florida cattle drivers who struggle to survive in the unforgiving environment of rural Florida. Today, cattle remains a large business in Florida, although most ranches are in the southern half of the peninsula.

To herd cattle, Florida cowboys generated a cracking sound by snapping their long whips. This technique earned them the nickname "cracker." Although the etymology of the term is ambiguous and perhaps has more than one root, today the term "cracker" is sometimes used to describe a person whose family has lived in Florida for many generations, but it can also be used as a pejorative term for an unsophisticated person.

The small community of **Enterprise** is located on the northern shores of Lake Monroe, which was a desirable location for early inhabitants and later European settlers, in part, because of its connection to the large St. Johns River system. Prior to the European era, Mayaca people lived in small villages here. The shell mounds (middens) they created offer a glimpse of what the Mayaca cooked and ate. A large midden along the shore of Lake Monroe in Enterprise provided evidence of the abundant food offered by the lake and surrounding land including snails, shellfish, alligators, and mammals such as deer. By the mid-1700s the Mayaca culture had been destroyed by European conquerors and their diseases. Sadly, the Enterprise midden no longer exists; by the early 1900s it had been destroyed, primarily used as road fill.

Enterprise's prime location, with access to both railway lines and steamboats, made it an important transportation hub and center of government in the 1800s. Its natural beauty attracted tourists, and the town's grand inn, the Brock House, hosted guests such as Harriet Beecher Stowe, President Ulysses S. Grant, and

President Grover Cleveland. Wealthy visitors looking for a bit of adventure and an escape from the cold northern winters congregated here. The city was destined for near economic ruin, however, after its population plummeted due to the back-to-back hits from the yellow fever epidemic of 1888 and hard freezes that destroyed the area's citrus groves in the 1890s.

Just 300 feet south of the C2C Trail is the **Enterprise Museum** (360 Main St., Enterprise). The small museum conveys the stories of Enterprise's past but also exhibits the work of contemporary local artists. The museum has limited hours of public access, so be sure to check its website (https://www.oldenterprise .org) for hours of operation and more information. Although the once thriving town of Enterprise is now a sleepy community, the Enterprise Preservation Society strives to safeguard the area's history and protect its rural charm.

OPTIONAL SPUR TRAIL: SPRING-TO-SPRING TRAIL TO DELEON SPRINGS

This 24-mile spur trail heads north from Gemini Springs Park to DeLeon Springs State Park.

The **Spring-to-Spring Trail** is a picturesque, well-designed trail that is part of Volusia County's growing network of trails. The C2C route follows the Spring-to-Spring Trail only for a few miles on the north side of Lake Monroe. For an adventure that heads farther north from Gemini Springs Park off the C2C, you can ride 24 miles on this scenic trail and have the benefit of visiting two parks that I highly recommend, Blue Springs State Park and DeLeon Springs State Park.

The trail names near Gemini Springs Park can be a bit confusing because of split routes and overlapping names (see map in "The Route: Need to Know"). The Spring-to-Spring Trail begins at Green Springs Park and heads west to Gemini Springs Park, and for this four-mile stretch, the C2C and the Spring-to-Spring Trail overlap. At Gemini Springs, the Spring-to-Spring Trail splits, and you can head either north or south. The northern portion travels

Spring-to-Spring Trail

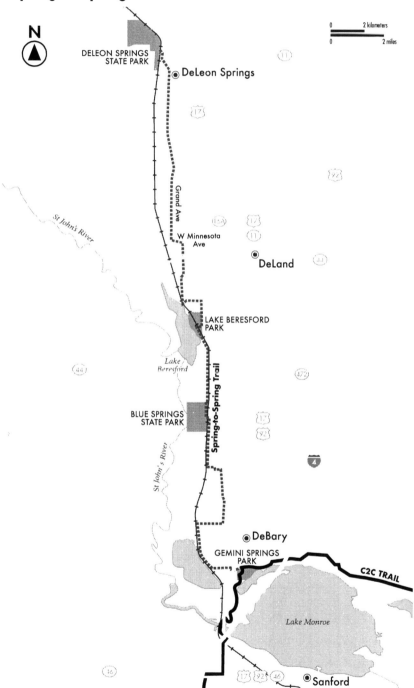

Optional 24-mile spur trail from Gemini Springs to DeLeon Springs

24 miles to DeLeon Springs, while the southern route takes you to Lake Monroe Park, which is the C2C route. In the following paragraphs, I describe the optional spur trail for the 24-mile portion of the Spring-to-Spring Trail between Gemini Springs and DeLeon Springs, all of which is separate from the C2C.

From Gemini Springs Park, head to the intersection of Dirksen Road and US 17-92 (S. Charles Richard Beall Blvd). The Spring-to-Spring Trail continues from the northwest corner of this intersection. Many miles of this trail are through forested land on an undulating, winding path. The hills on this spur are neither steep nor long, and the slight rolling changes in elevation make it fun to walk or ride.

At the time of publication, the Spring-to-Spring Trail was not yet complete, but the two remaining gaps can be navigated on roads. The 4.5-mile gap between Lake Beresford Park and 1995 W. Minnesota Avenue can be traversed using Fatio Road and then either Ridgewood Avenue or Grand Avenue as a north-south connector. Use caution crossing busy SR 44. The trail picks up again at the intersection of Grand Avenue and West Plymouth Avenue. Wide bike lanes on the north end of Grand Avenue take you to within one mile of DeLeon Springs State Park. For this final one-mile gap, travel through the low-traffic residential area to reach the park entrance.

In addition to offering many miles of picturesque, shaded paths, the trail travels to two excellent parks: **Blue Springs** and **DeLeon Springs**. Blue Springs is approximately nine miles north of Gemini Springs, while DeLeon Springs is at the end of the 24-mile spur. Both parks are part of the Florida State Park system and provide a variety of recreational activities in beautiful natural areas including kayaking, hiking, picnicking, swimming, and boat tours. Blue Springs State Park has camping facilities (tent and cabin), but DeLeon Springs State Park does not.

Both parks have large, pristine freshwater springs that are significantly larger than those at Gemini Springs; swimming is permitted in the springs of both parks (except in the winter at

Blue Springs when manatees are present). Swimming in a fresh-water spring in Florida during the summer is a wonderfully brisk experience. The spring water emanates from the aquifer at a refreshing 72° F throughout the year. Conversely, in chilly weather the constant temperature of the spring makes the water feel delightfully warm.

During winter cold snaps, **manatees** congregate at **Blue Springs**. Visit on a chilly day to get a close-up look at these impressive, gentle marine mammals. Manatees are herbivores and can grow to 12 feet long, often weighing more than 1,000 pounds. They move slowly and gracefully through the water using their wide tails and flippers. Manatees are usually solitary animals, but the lure of the warm spring water during a cold spell can bring hundreds together into Blue Springs. If you're lucky, you'll even see mothers and calves side by side. The lives of manatees are threatened by habitat loss, pollution, and collisions with boats. Park rangers work to educate people about these extraordinary animals and what they need to survive. Seeing manatees in the wild is an experience you'll never forget.

DeLeon Springs is locally known not only for its beautiful spring and surrounding natural area but also for the **Old Spanish Sugar Mill restaurant**. Although the restaurant offers a variety of food and a superb location situated by the spring, it is most famous for the novelty of cooking your own pancakes at your table. As the name suggests, a sugarcane mill once operated here using the flow of the spring water to turn its waterwheel. After you've been cycling, hiking, or paddling, it's a great place to stop for delicious nourishment.

The 4.5-mile DeLeon Springs Wild Persimmon hiking trail loop is a great wilderness trek, wandering through several differ-ent environments, including dense foliage of plants that thrive in wet ecosystems. The beauty of this area was appreciated by indig-enous people and European settlers alike. Naturalist William Bartram visited and documented the springs in 1774, as did John James Audubon in 1832. To entice tourists, the local community

The Old Spanish Sugar Mill restaurant at DeLeon Springs, situated by the spring, is a replica of the sugar mill that was built here in the 1830s.

changed the first English name for these springs, Spring Garden Run, to DeLeon Springs in the hopes that a perceived connection to Ponce de León and his quest for the fountain of youth would generate more buzz. In reality, the famed explorer never visited here.

The city center of **DeLand** is accessible via a variety of routes, many of which are suitable for bicycles, such as West Minnesota Avenue. At its closest point, downtown DeLand is three miles due east of the Spring-to-Spring Trail. DeLand is an eclectic mix of a historic town center, a small college town, and a growing art scene. Hotels and other lodging are available, as are a wide variety of specialty shops, restaurants, cafés, and bars. Woodland Boulevard, between the Stetson University campus to the north and Howry Avenue to the south, is the most vibrant part of the town.

Lake Beresford Park (2100 Fatio Rd., DeLand) abuts the Spring-to-Spring Trail about 5.5 miles southwest of DeLand and has a nice trailhead with parking, picnic pavilions, and restrooms. A 1.8-mile paved loop trail within the park connects to the

Spring-to-Spring Trail. At the time of publication, this park is at the southern end of the previously mentioned 4.5-mile trail gap.

This optional Spring-to-Spring Trail spur off the C2C is a very enjoyable excursion. The beautiful state parks along the route and the opportunity to spend an evening in DeLand's city center make a highly recommended trip.

TRAIL SECTION 3
SANFORD TO ALTAMONTE SPRINGS

SEMINOLE COUNTY, INCLUDING THE TOWNS OF LAKE MARY AND ALTAMONTE SPRINGS. OPTIONAL SPUR TRAIL TO SANFORD

Trail section length: 17 miles

Point A: Lake Monroe Wayside Park, 4150 US 17, Sanford (4.5 miles west of downtown Sanford near the intersection of I-4, US 17, and FL 15/West Seminole Boulevard)

Point B: Altamonte Springs San Sebastian Trailhead on the Seminole Wekiva Trail at SR 436, 0.25 mile east of the intersection of SR 436 and Laurel Street

Four-mile optional spur trail into the town center of Sanford

HIGHLIGHTS
Scenic path between Lake Mary and San Sebastian Trailhead
"Paint the Trail" artwork
Historic Sanford (via a four-mile spur trail)

Trail Section 3 – Sanford Wayside Park to Altamonte Springs

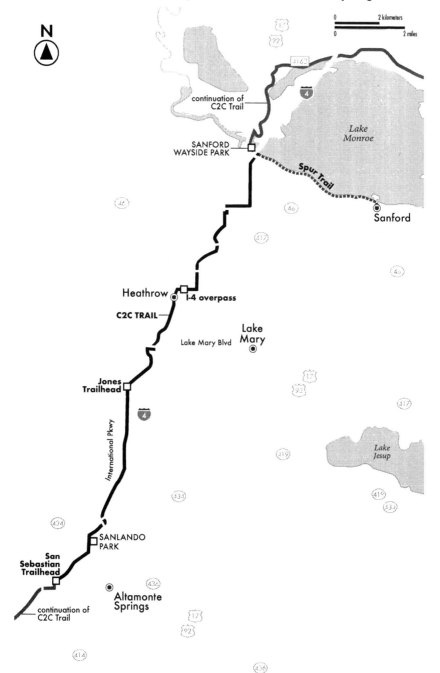

TRAILHEADS

Sanford Lake Monroe Wayside Park, 4150 US 17, Sanford

Fort Mellon Park, 600 East First St., Sanford; on-street parking. Also, street parking available on East Seminole Blvd. on the north side of Fort Mellon Park (near optional Sanford spur trail)

Lake Mary commercial parking lot, 1210 S. International Pkwy., Lake Mary

Jones Trailhead, 2993 Markham Woods Rd., Longwood

Seminole Softball Complex, 2200 North St., Altamonte Springs

Sanlando Park, 401 W. Highland St., Altamonte Springs

San Sebastian Trailhead, SR 436, a quarter mile east of Laurel St., Altamonte Springs

THE ROUTE: NEED TO KNOW

Over 10 miles of this segment follows a lovely portion of the popular Seminole Wekiva Trail. The northernmost tip of this section is less scenic and travels through a more congested commercial area for about four miles.

The history, waterfront, and lively nighttime restaurant and music scenes make the four-mile spur trail into Sanford worthwhile. See "Optional Spur Trail to Sanford" below.

The C2C crosses the St. Johns River alongside US 17 at the western edge of Lake Monroe. There is a wide protected path for cyclists and pedestrians on the bridge. Lake Monroe Wayside Park, where Trail Section 3 begins, is at the southern end of the bridge, just west of the major intersection of I-4 and US 17. The trail splits at this intersection. Travel east from this intersection on the path alongside the lake (parallel to FL 15/West Seminole Boulevard) to ride the spur route to Sanford. The main C2C route to Altamonte Springs heads south from this intersection on the path parallel to Monroe Road/US 17. It's a good place to verify that you are on the right path.

At the time of publication, work is progressing toward the completion of **a 27-mile loop bicycle route that will encircle Lake Monroe**. This will enable C2C riders to choose the side of the lake they wish to travel and will provide the option to incorporate the entire loop as a ride. Currently, 23 miles of the loop trail are complete; the missing piece is along Celery Avenue between downtown Sanford and East Lake Mary Boulevard. This missing segment is projected to be completed in 2024. North of Lake Monroe, the loop trail is on the existing C2C path. The existing four-mile spur trail into Sanford along the south side of the lake is also part of the loop.

Between Lake Monroe Wayside Park and the H.E. Thomas, Jr. Parkway, the C2C path is essentially a **4.5-mile connector section** built adjacent to roadways to link the Spring-to-Spring Trail to the Seminole Wekiva Trail. Some portions feel more like a wide sidewalk than a bicycling path. The approximately two-mile section of the C2C that runs between First Street in Sanford to the H.E. Thomas, Jr. Parkway is in a busy commercial area that entails intersections with motorized traffic. One advantage to this high-traffic area is the variety of convenience stores and restaurants near the trail. Be particularly vigilant about car traffic in this vicinity.

Along this trail segment, the C2C **crosses Interstate 4** via a pedestrian/bicycle overpass. This overpass connects the Seminole Wekiva Trail (parallel to International Parkway on the west side of I-4) to the Rhinehart bicycle path (parallel to Rhinehart Rd. on the east side of I-4). Traveling in either direction, you must **make a 90-degree turn** to reach the overpass, and the **turn can be easy to miss**. To find the overpass:

If heading **east to west on the C2C**, and heading south on the Rhinehart Road parallel trail, the I-4 overpass is reached by turning right (west) at the traffic-signal intersection with the road named "Postal Dist. Ctr." This is 0.5 mile south of H.E. Thomas, Jr. Parkway.

If heading **west to east on the C2C**, and therefore heading north on the Seminole Wekiva Trail, the right turn to the I-4 overpass is 1.8 miles north of the Lake Mary Boulevard intersection underpass. An office park at 901 International Parkway is approximately 300 feet south of the turn.

RECOMMENDED WALKS

A lovely one-mile walk along the spur trail's **Sanford Riverwalk** offers broad views of Lake Monroe. Start at **Fort Mellon Park** and walk along the south shore of Lake Monroe toward North French Avenue. Head out to the **Monroe Harbor Marina** for close-up looks of sailboats and perhaps lunch at a nice seafood restaurant. This walk also takes you past Sanford's **Veterans' Memorial Park** (100 E. Seminole Blvd.), which juts out into Lake Monroe. Monuments and engraved bricks are dedicated to those who served in the country's armed forces.

The entire length of the Sanford riverside trail between Fort Mellon Park and the I-4/FL 15/US 17 intersection is four miles.

View of Lake Monroe along Sanford's Riverwalk

Head west from the Sanford Marina on the trail and you will find the shoreline populated with fishermen, walkers, joggers, and cyclists. In addition to the views of Lake Monroe, walkers will enjoy a close-up look at shoreline vegetation and the animals that make this area home such as Great Blue Herons and Ospreys. The old pilings jutting out of the water are remnants of steamboat docks from a long-past era.

West of I-4, the portion of the C2C path that incorporates the **Seminole Wekiva Trail** has gorgeous tree-lined sections, with several trailheads and facilities. In particular, the 7.5 miles of the C2C between Lake Mary Boulevard in the north and San Sebastian Trailhead in the south are excellent for walking. You'll also be entertained by the "Paint the Trail" work by artist Jeff Sonksen along the trail (see "Local Culture" below). The **Jones Trailhead** is a good access point for this part of the trail. Because of the excellent trail conditions, this section can be busy with both cyclists and walkers, particularly on weekends.

LOCAL CULTURE

The four-mile Sanford spur trail leads you into historic downtown Sanford. This is a worthy stop for views of Lake Monroe and for the town's restaurants, breweries, and historic buildings. For details, see "Optional Spur Trail to Sanford" below.

Discover the work of **"Paint the Trail"** artist Jeff Sonksen along the C2C/Seminole Wekiva Trail in **Longwood**. You will enjoy seeing hundreds of images he has painted on fences bordering the trail, many of which are inspired by pop culture. Sonksen started his "Paint the Trail" movement in 2012 when he painted a few images on his parents' privacy fence. His artistic creations caught the attention of trail users and neighbors, and Sonksen was asked to paint more fences. His work crops up sporadically over a couple of miles between the Jones Trailhead on Long Pond Road and E. E. Williamson Road. Keep an eye out for it on both sides of the trail. Sonksen's creations have expanded beyond pop culture to include images of endangered species, historical figures,

Jeff Sonksen's "Paint the Trail" project enlivens the C2C with artwork.

and local celebrities. Stop to get a close look and take photographs. The face cutout spot based on Grant Wood's *American Gothic* work, including the farmhouse in the background, is a fun place for snapshots.

Trail Section 3 is entirely in Seminole County, whose motto is "Florida's Natural Choice." The county's 15-mile distance from the city of Orlando protected it from some of the rampant suburban sprawl that consumed parts of Orange County during the 1950s through the 1980s. One of the benefits of this delayed growth is Seminole County's improved planning processes, which preserved large swaths of land and created many outdoor recreational facilities. Sanlando Softball Complex (2200 North St., Altamonte Springs) and the neighboring Sanlando Park (401 W. Highland St., Altamonte Springs), both of which are adjacent to the C2C, are good examples of the county's commitment to recreational activities. These parks also provide a nice respite for trail users, with benches, pavilions, restrooms, and water fountains.

The C2C travels through the towns of **Lake Mary** and **Altamonte Springs** but does not intersect with either town's central business districts. Instead, trail users see the quieter side of these towns where residents live and play.

NATURE

The St. Johns River and Lake Monroe provide a bountiful habitat for fish and, consequently, for the birds that consume fish, such as Ospreys, Bald Eagles, and a variety of herons and egrets. In the spring, you may even see these birds nesting near the lakeshore. **Osprey** and **Bald Eagle** nests must accommodate both the parents and the fast-growing babies, so they can be quite large. Mated pairs of both species often return to a nest year after year, reinforcing and enlarging it. Because of similarities between these species, Ospreys are sometimes mistakenly identified as eagles. For a quick way to tell them apart, look at the bird's chest. A Bald Eagle's chest is dark brown, while an Osprey's chest is mostly white. And while adult birds of both species have white on their heads, only adult Bald Eagles have the distinctive all-white tail.

Less than a half mile from the C2C (and directly on the Sanford spur trail) is the **Central Florida Zoo & Botanical Gardens** (3755 W. Seminole Blvd., Sanford). This 100-acre facility aims to inspire individuals to learn about and protect wildlife. In addition to providing educational and observational opportunities centered on the 300-plus resident animals, there is an aerial zip line, butterfly garden, and eatery. For more information, see https://www .centralfloridazoo.org.

Seminole County is also home to **Florida black bears** (*Ursus americanus floridanus*). Visitors are unlikely to see one, but bears occasionally stray into populated areas. Sometimes, they remain close but out of sight, sitting high up in trees. Female black bears may weigh up to 200 pounds, and a full-grown male can weight twice as much. Vegetation, such as berries and nuts, make up most of their diet, although these bears also eat bugs and sometimes

Alligators (*Alligator mississippiensis*)

Alligators populate Central Florida's lakes, ponds, and rivers. They are unlikely to be encountered on the asphalt C2C path, but if you have time to stop and look, you will likely see at least one on your travels. Scan the water's surface and search for a dark head with protruding eyes. The body typically isn't seen unless the gator is actively swimming or it is resting in shallow water or on shore. Swimming gators can sink slowly down into the water barely making a ripple. Or if startled, they can make a frightful ruckus.

In Central Florida, if you see these reptiles, note that they are alligators, not crocodiles. Alligators typically prefer freshwater lakes or rivers, while crocodiles are adapted to live equally in either freshwater or saltwater environments. The distinct environment of the Everglades in the southern tip of Florida makes it the only place on earth where alligators and crocodiles share a habitat. The easiest way to tell an alligator from a crocodile is the shape of their snout. The shape of an alligator's snout is broad and similar to a "U," while crocodiles have pointed snouts shaped more like a "V."

Never feed an alligator, being fed by humans makes these predators unafraid of people and causes them to associate humans with food, leading to potentially deadly interactions. If you do see one, keep a safe distance away; on land, alligators can lunge for a short distance at speeds up to 30 miles per hour.

An alligator basks in the sun.

other animals. In suburban Florida, black bears have been known to rummage through garbage containers foraging for food. This has led to dangerous interactions with people and pets. Seminole County has been proactive in distributing bear-resistant garbage containers to discourage this behavior.

HISTORICAL NOTES

Historically, the St. Johns River and many of the waterways of Florida have been a veritable paradise for birds, fish, and game. The abundance of wading birds such as egrets and herons led to the infamous feather trade of the late 1800s, in which millions of birds were killed for their plumage (the feathers were particularly prized for making fashionable hats). Florida became a prime location for plumage hunters, who quickly decimated bird populations. The wispy, bright white feathers of Snowy Egrets were particularly in demand. The Florida Audubon Society was founded in 1900 to protect birds and, with the assistance of many activists, helped to pass a law in 1901 that outlawed plume hunting in the state.

Celery City

Sanford earned the nickname "Celery City" for the agricultural success of celery crops in the area during the 20th century, a reference you'll continue to see today. In addition to growing celery and other crops, Sanford was one of the largest vegetable shipping centers in the United States. Celery farming replaced many of the citrus groves in the area after acres of citrus trees were killed in the severe freezes of 1894 and 1895. Today's celery crop in Florida is grown primarily in muck farms in South Florida near Lake Okeechobee (close to the Everglades). Modern Sanford entrepreneurs pay homage to this nickname, and you'll find small businesses in the heart of Sanford such as Celery City Brewing and Celery City Cigars.

Sanford Spur Trail

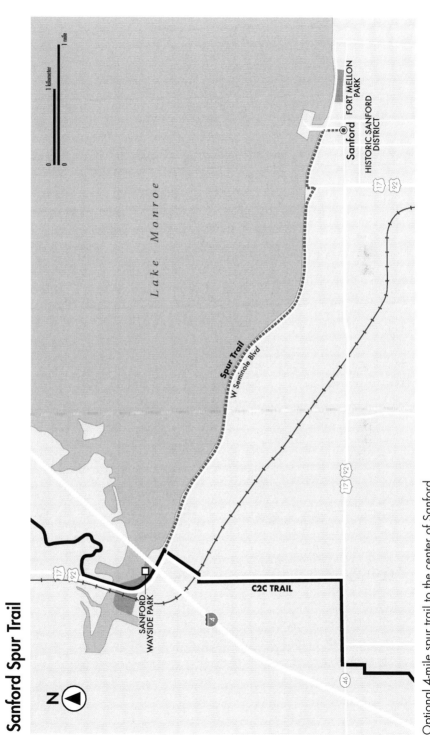

N

Lake Monroe

Spur Trail
W Seminole Blvd

SANFORD
WAYSIDE PARK

C2C TRAIL

FORT MELLON
PARK

Sanford

HISTORIC SANFORD
DISTRICT

17 92

17 92

46

0   1 kilometer

0   1 mile

Optional 4-mile spur trail to the center of Sanford

OPTIONAL SPUR TRAIL TO SANFORD

Travel a short way off the C2C to explore the lakeside town of Sanford.

On the southwest shore of Lake Monroe, at the intersection of I-4 and US 17, a four-mile path parallel to SR 15 leads along the lakeshore into the town center of Sanford. Enjoy the waterfront parks and marina, then head a few blocks south to explore the city and its neighborhoods.

Sanford has many good restaurants, several breweries, and a variety of live music venues. It is a small city perhaps best enjoyed in the evenings or at night when these establishments are lively, but several restaurants are open for breakfast and lunch. The town also hosts numerous art and music festivals. Explore the old section of downtown, generally east of South Oak Avenue and north of Fifth Street, to find craft breweries, eateries, art galleries, street festivities, and more.

Florida's definition of "old" differs considerably from that of Europe, Asia, or even the northeastern United States. But Sanford successfully combines its historic character with newfound vibrancy. Eight locations within the city are listed on the National Register of Historic Places. Fortunately, the town has been able to maintain these historical buildings while attracting new enterprises and residents. Sanford's old houses encompass a variety of styles, including Folk Victorian, Arts and Crafts, and even Sears home kits.

Although the Sanford area was well known for its commercial agriculture, its previous official name, "Mellonville," was not related to the fruit. Rather, the name was bestowed in remembrance of Captain Charles Mellon, who died here in a fight against the Seminole Tribe in 1837. A fort had been established by the lake in 1836 due to its strategic location. Native Seminoles, continuing to resist their forced removal from Florida, attacked the fort during the Second Seminole War, and Captain Mellon was the sole army casualty. Fort Mellon was named in his memory, as was the nearby

Downtown Sanford

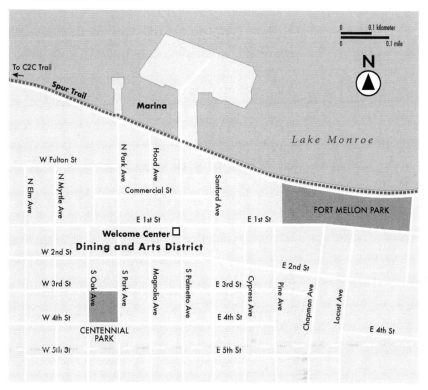

settlement. Mellonville's name was later changed to Sanford to honor Henry S. Sanford, a prominent businessman and advocate for the town's development in the late 1800s.

Sanford owes its rich history to its exceptional location. Lake Monroe, part of the 310-mile-long St. Johns River, gave Sanford shipping access to the Atlantic Ocean via the port city of Jacksonville. Railways traversing the state, including the Orange Belt Railway, connected Sanford to the west coast of Florida. In the mid-1800s, when transportation was a major hurdle to commercial businesses, access to boats and trains made Sanford a hub of activity.

Sanford Marina on the shores of Lake Monroe

At one time, nearly 150 **steamboats** operated on the river, connecting the towns of Sanford, Palatka, and Jacksonville. From the 1830s to the 1920s, these ships were an efficient and economical way to transport people and goods in the state. The steamboat era was destined to end, however, with the construction of improved railways and new roads for the newly invented automobile. In 1912, Henry Flagler's Florida East Coast Railway was completed, running from Jacksonville all the way to Florida's southern tip at Key West. Along the south shore of Lake Monroe, there are still a few remnants of pilings from the old steamboat docks. In a nod to these bygone days, the St. Johns Rivership Co. operates lunch and dinner cruises on a paddleboat that cruises the St. Johns River, departing from the Sanford Marina (433 N. Palmetto Ave.).

For a lively evening, head to Sanford's Historic District. Although the actual historic district is quite large, most of the action is in the blocks bordered by First Street, Sanford Avenue, Sixth Street, and Elm Avenue. Live music, breweries, restaurants (both casual and upscale), and funky shops make this an interesting scene at night. The Old Jailhouse restaurant on Palmetto Avenue is in the building that was Sanford's jail until 1959. Hollerbach's Willow Tree Café, an institution on First Avenue, offers authentic German food and music.

For baseball fans, the **Historic Sanford Memorial Stadium** (1201 Mellonville Ave.) is situated less than a mile from the center of Sanford and easily accessible by riding or walking through quiet neighborhood streets. The current stadium was built in 1951, and although substantially refurbished, it retains its charm and historical feel. It currently hosts games for the Florida Collegiate Summer League but has a storied past as the Spring Training home for the Atlanta Braves and the New York Giants.

A proposed bicycle route south of Lake Monroe heading east from Sanford will eventually complete a 27-mile route around the lake. See "The Route: Need to Know" above for more information about this loop.

There is limited lodging (primarily boutique) in the historic Sanford district, but several hotels are located near the C2C at the intersection of I-4 and SR 46.

TRAIL SECTION 4
ALTAMONTE SPRINGS TO CLERMONT

SEMINOLE, ORANGE, AND LAKE COUNTIES, INCLUDING THE TOWNS OF WINTER GARDEN AND OAKLAND

Trail section length: 31 miles
Point A: Altamonte Springs San Sebastian Trailhead on the
    Seminole Wekiva Trail, 0.25 mile east of the intersection of
    SR 436 and Laurel St.
Point B: Clermont Waterfront Park, 330 Third St., Clermont

HIGHLIGHTS
Historic and lively downtown Winter Garden
Tree-covered pleasant cycling path
Oakland Nature Preserve
Clermont Waterfront Park & Historic Village
Hills!

Trail Section 4 – Altamonte Springs to Clermont

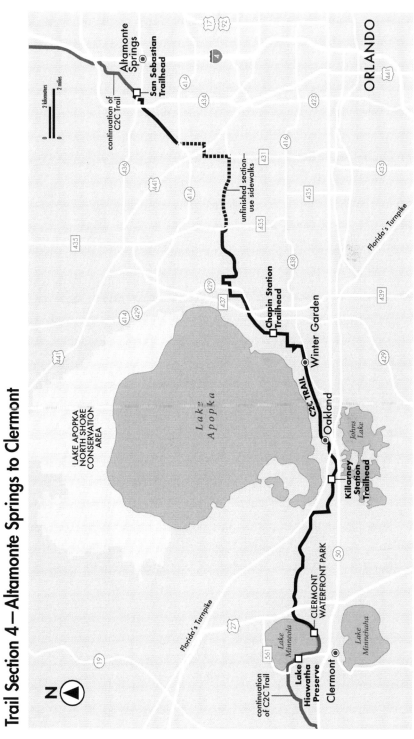

TRAILHEADS

San Sebastian Trailhead, SR 436, just east of the intersection of
   Laurel St.
Apopka Vineland Outpost, 5794 N. Apopka Vineland Rd.,
   Orlando
Chapin Station, 501 Crown Point Cross Rd., Winter Garden
Winter Garden Station, 455 East Plant St., Winter Garden
Oakland, 220 N. Tubb St., Oakland
Killarney Station, 17914 SR 438, Winter Garden
Minneola Trailhead Park, 315 Madison St., Minneola
Clermont Waterfront Park, 330 Third St., Clermont

THE ROUTE: NEED TO KNOW

On this segment of the C2C you will travel along the West Orange
Trail (Orange County) and the South Lake Trail (Lake County,
also called the Minneola Scenic Trail). Much of this segment is
well marked and easy to follow, but there are a few sections that
require special attention.

Immediately south of the San Sebastian Trailhead near SR
436, the trail navigates through a commercial/retail area with two
busy intersections. Both intersections have traffic signals. The first
is where C2C crosses SR 436 at the traffic-signaled intersection
at Laurel Street. The second busy intersection is at SR 434 and
Orange Avenue. Plans to construct trail tunnels at each of these
intersections are in progress.

At the time of publication, there is a **5.5-mile gap** in the trail
between the **Seminole Wekiva Trail** and the **West Orange Trail**.
To cross this gap, cyclists have found the following route, and
many use the sidewalks unless traveling when car traffic is light:

Traveling east to west on the C2C, and therefore south on
the Seminole Wekiva Trail: At the (busy) intersection of Bear
Lake Road, Maitland Boulevard (SR 414), and Rose Avenue, cross
Maitland Boulevard and go south on Rose Avenue for one mile.
Turn right (west) on Beggs Road for 0.5 mile. Turn left (south)
onto North Pine Hills Road for one mile. Turn right (west) on to

Orange County Gap Route

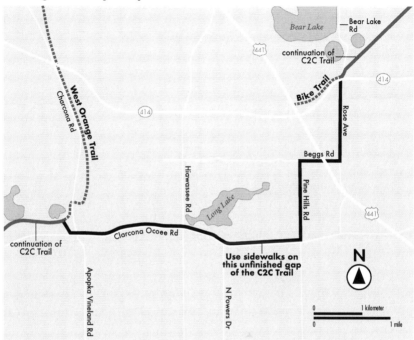

Navigating the 5.5-mile trail gap in Orange County. Sidewalks are available.

Clarcona Ocoee Road and travel 3.1 miles. After about two miles on Clarcona Ocoee Road, bicycle lanes are available. The right-hand turn onto the spur path to the West Orange Trail is 500 feet after crossing North Apopka Vineland Road. When the 800-foot spur path reaches the West Orange Trail at a "T" intersection, turn left, and continue on the trail.

Traveling west to east on the C2C, and therefore east on the West Orange Trail: Take a (currently unmarked) right-hand turn onto a spur trail 1.8 miles after you pass the small trailhead parking lot at Ingram Road. If you reach the Apopka Vineland Outpost and the Chùa Báo Ân Buddhist Temple on your right, you've gone too far. This short spur path (800 feet) heads south to Clarcona

73

Ocoee Road. Turn east/left onto Clarcona Ocoee Road on the sidewalks or use the bicycle lanes, but be aware that the bicycle lanes currently end after about a mile. After traveling three miles on Clarcona Ocoee Road, turn left (north) on North Pine Hills Road for one mile. Turn right (east) on Beggs Road for 0.5 mile. Turn left (north) onto Rose Avenue. After one mile, at the intersection of Rose Avenue, Bear Lake Avenue, and Maitland Boulevard, the C2C path resumes on the northeast corner of the intersection.

The intersection of the **West Orange Trail** and **Lulu Creek Trail** can be slightly confusing. About 0.8 mile northeast of the Winter Garden Station Trailhead, the C2C/West Orange Trail makes a 90-degree turn on the north side of East Division Street, where it abuts the short Lulu Creek Trail. Do not take the Lulu Creek Trail.

The Lake County section of the C2C incorporates regional trails named the Lake Minneola Scenic Trail and the South Lake Trail, and signage uses these regional names.

At the **Hancock Road intersection** in Clermont, the C2C uses a short portion (1,000 feet) of trail parallel to Hancock Road. Be attentive here, and do not stay on the Hancock Road parallel trail, which heads away from the C2C both north and south. Cross Hancock Road and stay parallel to Old Highway 50 in an east-west direction.

Camping is available at Clarcona Horse Park (3535 Damon Rd., Apopka), approximately 1.5 miles from the C2C, easily accessed on a spur trail.

RECOMMENDED WALKS

Many pleasant and beautiful places to walk can be found on this segment of the trail. Numerous trailheads also make these walks very accessible and easy to plan. Several of the walks I describe below can be combined.

The 1.5 miles between the **Apopka Vineland Outpost** (5794 N. Apopka Vineland Rd.) and the C2C intersection with Clark Road at 9400 Clarcona Ocoee Road are a lovely stretch of a mostly tree-lined path with a slight elevation change. There is parking at the Apopka Vineland Outpost but no parking or facilities at the Clark Road intersection.

Enjoy walking the 3.8-mile section between the **West Orange Trail Winter Garden Station** (455 E. Plant St.) and the **Oakland Nature Preserve** (747 Machete Tr., Oakland). This is a delightful stretch that includes the heart of historic Winter Garden; interesting architecture; large shade trees; and facilities for picnics, restrooms, and water. A large sign from the trail directs you to the entrance of the Oakland Nature Preserve. Visit the preserve's education center for information about the flora and fauna of the area as well as maps of the multiple short trails on the property. The preserve's unpaved trails are well marked and can be combined for approximately two miles of woodland hiking or through the elevated sandhill restoration area. A 0.7-mile boardwalk meanders through a forested wetland out to Lake Apopka. For more information, see the "Nature" section below.

The trail passes through the center of Winter Garden, a vibrant state-designated Trail Town.

For a shorter walk (0.8 mile) to the **Oakland Nature Preserve** (747 Machete Tr.), start in the center of **Oakland** at the parking lot near the **Art and Heritage Center** (220 N. Tubb St.). This section of the C2C is well traveled by other walkers and cyclists.

Between **Minneola Trailhead Park** (315 Madison St., Minneola) to **Clermont Waterfront Park** (330 Third St., Clermont) is a 1.6-mile stretch of the C2C that travels along the southeast shore of Lake Minneola to a delightfully wooded, elevated area adjacent to the south side of Minneola Trailhead Park.

LOCAL CULTURE

From the Apopka Vineland Outpost to the Killarney Station, the C2C follows the **West Orange Trail**, one of the early long-distance shared-use trails developed in Central Florida. The trail is built on the former narrow-gauge train line, the Orange Belt Railway, which once connected Sanford to St. Petersburg. The surrounding region was primarily agricultural through the 1900s. Over the past several decades, orange groves have been gradually replaced with subdivisions and commercial development. But there is much to enjoy, and the oak tree canopy and rolling hills of the area add to its appeal.

Much of the rural and small-town feel of this area has been preserved along the C2C. Historic sites along the route coupled with modern amenities make this an enjoyable trail segment to ride and walk. Many of the trailheads, including Chapin Station, Winter Garden Station, and Killarney Station, are well designed and provide trail users with a pleasant respite, including picnic areas, water, restrooms, and playgrounds surrounded by trees. The popularity of this trail among locals is testament to its charm.

The town center of **Winter Garden** owes much of its wildly successful revitalization to the West Orange Trail, the influx of trail users, and good city management. In the heart of the town, the C2C travels down the middle of Plant Street, passing numerous restaurants, shops, and breweries. The town hosts several annual festivals, live music on weekends, a large weekly farmers' market, and festive holiday displays. The unique Edgewater Inn (99 W. Plant St.) was built in 1927, then renovated and reopened in 2003, and the gracious feel of the building endures. Stop by the lobby to soak in the ambiance of a long-ago era, or enjoy a scoop of ice cream from the neighboring old-fashioned ice cream parlor.

Winter Garden's efforts to preserve its architecture and remember its past are successful in part through the efforts of the Winter Garden Heritage Foundation. The Foundation operates

Lake Apopka

Lake Apopka is Florida's fourth largest lake, and in the 1940s it was a major attraction for bass fishermen from around the United States. At that time, over 20 fish camps lined the shores of the lake, and Winter Garden was a center of activity for these visitors. However, human activity in and near the lake from the 1940s to the 1980s proved to be disastrous. The lake level was lowered for the purposes of farming the northern shore, and farming practices released harmful chemicals and nutrients. Later, toxic spills by a pesticide manufacturer added to the pollution and made the lake unsafe for both wildlife and people.

In 1996, the Lake Apopka Restoration Act was passed, which provided funding to revert surrounding areas to wetlands, reduce contaminants in the soil, and eliminate phosphorus runoff from farms. The massive efforts to restore the lake were successful, and now, wildlife, particularly fish, birds, and alligators, once again flourishes here. In 2014, the north shore of Lake Apopka was opened to the public with bicycle and hiking trails as well as a one-way 11-mile wildlife drive for cars. To get a good look at Lake Apopka, visit Newton Park in Winter Garden or take the boardwalk from the Oakland Nature Preserve.

the **Heritage Museum** (1 N. Main St.). You can't miss the bright yellow **train caboose** parked at the entrance to the museum along the C2C. The small museum tells the story of the region's past, including the Timucuan settlement on Lake Apopka, early local pioneers, citrus growers of the past century, and notable community leaders. The museum also houses an appealing and varied collection of citrus crate label artwork.

The **Central Florida Railroad Museum** (101 S. Boyd St.) is located one block south of the C2C in an actual railroad depot built in 1913. It's a small museum crammed full of railroad memorabilia such as dining car china, signs, train lanterns, and early radio equipment.

Oakland's tiny town center borders the trail, where you'll find municipal buildings and trail-friendly amenities. Be sure to stop by here and spend a few minutes strolling under the shaded oak trees, relaxing at the picnic tables, and discovering the picturesque **historic town hall and post office** just a few steps away from the trail. The city strives to incorporate the trail as part of its culture

Oakland's Town Hall and the adjacent park make a picturesque rest stop.

and generously provides water fountains and restrooms to trail users.

The **Healthy West Orange Arts and Heritage Center at the Town of Oakland** (126 W. Petris Ave.) encourages residents to live a healthy lifestyle and actively encourages outdoor exercise such as bicycling, running, walking, and skating. Its role as a heritage center is evident in the displays of historical artifacts as well as contemporary art exhibits. Stop here to rest on the benches situated under a wide tree canopy and to enjoy the opportunity to encounter a bit of Oakland's charm.

Clermont's waterfront revival is partially indebted to the success of outdoor recreation opportunities of the area, including the C2C/West Orange Trail. **Clermont Waterfront Park**, on the south shore of **Lake Minneola**, is host to various sporting events but also provides a lovely place for residents and visitors to relax, enjoy the lake, and cool off at the splash pad. The city has embraced triathlons and bicycling events for their recreational value and the income they bring to the area. Many of these events, such as the annual Great Clermont Triathlon and the Florida Freewheelers Horrible Hundred bicycle ride, are staged at the Waterfront Park.

The south shore of Lake Minneola is also home to **Clermont's Historic Village Museum** (490 West Ave.). Included in the small village are historic homes, a re-created one-room schoolhouse, a train depot, and a World War II museum. Wander through the village for a step back in time. The organization's goal is to preserve and educate visitors about Clermont's pioneering past.

Florida's climate makes this a perfect place for year-round athletic training, and you'll find many runners and cyclists in the area. The **National Training Center** (1935 Don Wickham Dr., Clermont) is a high-level sports and fitness training center with a focus on swimmers, triathletes, and runners. Visiting athletes and local fitness enthusiasts train here. The hills of the Clermont area are a particular draw to active Floridians looking for a challenge.

Keep your eyes open while traveling east of Clermont, and you may see a tall spire. This is the 226-foot-tall **Florida Citrus**

Tower, built in 1956. An enclosed observation deck at the top of the tower offers visitors a panoramic view. Originally, the tower overlooked the endless citrus groves and lakes of the region. Now, with many citrus groves gone, the scene includes the expanse of the growing region's subdivisions and commercial development but also its lakes and, interestingly, a look at the Lake Wales Ridge (see box insert "Lake Wales Ridge").

NATURE

One mile north of Winter Garden's Plant Street town center is **Newton Park** (31 W. Garden Ave., Winter Garden). This park is known for its expansive views of Lake Apopka, opportunities for observing wildlife, and wide sunset vistas. Alligators, Ospreys, gallinules, limpkins, anhinga, egrets, and herons are common here, and lucky observers may find Snail Kites, an endangered raptor species that feeds only on snails. Cycle or walk the quiet residential streets in the neighborhood north of Plant Street to reach Newton Park from the C2C.

A real treasure along the C2C is the **Oakland Nature Preserve** (747 Machete Tr., Oakland). The preserve safeguards 130 acres of forested wetland and upland sandhill ecosystems. The education center has an inviting row of rocking chairs that overlook a field of native wildflowers, trees, and shrubs. Enjoy exploring this natural environment on two miles of hiking trails and a 0.7-mile boardwalk heading out to the edge of Lake Apopka. An ongoing project at the Preserve is the restoration of a 20-acre sandhill pine habitat that was cleared in the 1800s for agriculture. Since the restoration project began, the Preserve reports an extraordinary increase in native species of birds, mammals, and reptiles, including threatened gopher tortoises.

The Preserve's large, covered pavilion at the end of the boardwalk on Lake Apopka is an opportune place to relax and look for wildlife. Egrets, herons, woodpeckers, alligators, anoles, and turtles all call this area home. In late summer and fall, swamp hibiscus (*Hibiscus coccineus*, also called rose mallow and swamp mallow) put

The Oakland Nature Preserve is a beautiful place to explore. Plan a stop here to walk through the Preserve and perhaps fill up your water bottles or relax on the rocking chairs at the Education Center.

on a colorful show of large red blooms. These stunning flowers attract butterflies, bees, and birds. Bicycles are not permitted on the trails or boardwalk. Restrooms and water fountains are available at the education center.

Along this section of the C2C, between Oakland and Clermont, you'll cross the **Lake Wales Ridge**, a 150-mile-long sand ridge of scrub habitat (see box below). This sand ridge creates hillier riding than in most parts of the Florida peninsula, but you may enjoy the change in geology. Although the hills can provide a bit of a challenge, they are not too daunting. The hilliest section on the C2C is between the Killarney Station Trailhead and the Clermont waterfront. The elevation of the C2C peaks out at about 150 feet above sea level.

Vast pine forests of the area were harvested by the timber and turpentine industries. On cleared land that was suitable for

Lake Wales Ridge

Geologically, Florida's peninsula has been subject to the rise and fall of sea levels over the eons. About 2 million years ago, most of the peninsula was on the ocean floor, except for a line of islands along what is now known as the Lake Wales Ridge. Running north-south for approximately 150 miles, the sand ridge extends into Highlands, Polk, Osceola, Orange, and Lake Counties. The highest point of the ridge is Sugarloaf Mountain in Clermont, 312 feet (95 meters) above sea level. Sugarloaf is also the highest point on the Florida peninsula, making it a favorite training spot for cyclists, runners, and triathletes. The highest elevation in the state is much farther north: Britton Hill, at 345 feet above sea level, is 400 miles away in the state's northwest panhandle.

While the habitat of the Lake Wales Ridge varies widely, it is perhaps best known for its dry scrublands. Scrub habitat is important to species such as the Florida Scrub Jay, a threatened bird species found only in the State of Florida. Gopher tortoises also call scrub habitat their home. Plants such as sand pines, scrub oaks, and slash pines are well adapted to this sandy well-drained area, which had been coastal sand dunes during the Pleistocene epoch. Portions of the Lake Wales Ridge are preserved by government agencies as refuges and parks.

agriculture, citrus trees were often planted. In the 1980s, however, several severe freezes devasted the citrus trees, and many citrus growers sold land to housing developers. Most of the commercial citrus groves are now in the more southern parts of the state.

Clermont Waterfront Park provides a beautiful place to stop and relax to enjoy the shore of **Lake Minneola**. A sand beach, picnic pavilions, restrooms, open spaces, and a splash pad encourage visitors and residents alike to stop and enjoy this park. Lake Minneola is safe for swimming, although it is best to keep an eye out for alligators, especially during twilight or at night.

The brownish color of Lake Minneola is common in freshwater lakes and streams in Florida. The brown tinge is caused when organic material such as tree bark, roots, and leaves (which contain tannins) break down and seep into the water. The brown tea-stain color from this natural process is not an indication of pollution. However, Florida's lakes have come under immense ecological pressure due to stormwater debris and pollutants, phosphorus runoff from agriculture and lawns, and pesticide use. Water management districts and programs such as Florida Lakewatch strive to educate individuals about water pollution and ways to conserve and protect our valuable water resources.

HISTORICAL NOTES

What is now known as Orange County, Florida, was once called **Mosquito County**, and for good reason: mosquitos love Florida's hot and humid climate. In 1845, when Florida became the 27th state of the United States, the name was changed to Orange County, in part, to reflect the state's thriving citrus industry but undoubtably because the new name was more alluring and tourist friendly.

Like much of this region, the C2C towns of Ocoee, Oakland, and Winter Garden were citrus and agricultural hubs during the second half of the 1800s. Railroads built in the late 1800s connected these towns to other parts of Florida, drawing more settlers to the area. The combination of increased agricultural production with access to new markets via the railways was a recipe for early economic success of these towns.

Oakland's history can be explored at the **Healthy West Orange Arts and Heritage Center** in the town of Oakland (126 W. Petris Ave.). Long before Orlando became the region's business and political center, Oakland was the core of commercial activity. Oakland's first US Post Office opened in 1860, and for

Signage along the West Orange Trail segment of the C2C

several years, it was the only operational post office in present-day Orange County. The section of the Orange Belt Railway connecting Oakland to Lake Apopka and north to Lake Monroe at Sanford was completed in 1886. Peter Demens, the Russian-born businessman (born Petrovitch A. Demenscheff), who was instrumental in developing the Orange Belt Railway, was the elected as the first mayor of Oakland in 1891. Demens wanted to name this town St. Petersburg after his hometown in Russia, but the name of Oakland was chosen in tribute to the town's large and stately oak trees. Demens's aspiration for a town named St. Petersburg was eventually realized; in 1903, a thriving coastal town in Pinellas County was named to honor him and his Russian heritage: St. Petersburg, Florida.

The growth of Oakland coincided with the development of neighboring towns of Winter Garden and Clermont, which also benefited from the railroad connections and agricultural enterprises. Farmers found success with plants other than citrus, including commercially successful tomato crops.

This area was strongly affected by the early "Big Freeze" of 1894–1895. Disastrous to citrus groves and growers, it took more than 15 years after the freeze for production to return to previous levels. Another consequence of the freeze was plummeting real estate prices, as many farmers sold their land and moved away. Those who stayed endured years of financial hardship. For a while, work turned away from citrus toward lumber and turpentine enterprises.

Groveland, originally named Taylorville, was primarily a lumber- and turpentine-producing town of the late 19th century. Town leaders changed the name to Groveland in 1911 with an eye toward attracting land buyers and citrus farmers to the town. By the 1940s, it was primarily a citrus-producing town and remained so until once again, hard freezes destroyed groves, this time in the 1980s. Groveland was also at the center of the infamous and horrific events of 1949 when four Black men were falsely accused of raping a white woman (see box below).

Today, the towns of Oakland, Winter Garden, and Clermont have changed dramatically from their roots as agricultural and timber towns. Housing and commercial developments have been built to meet the needs of a burgeoning population, many of whom move to Florida for the warm weather and recreational or economic opportunities. Continued building growth can be seen

The Dark Past of Central Florida

A number of small towns in rural Central Florida have a troubled history of racial bigotry and injustice. The city of Ocoee was the site of the horrific 1920 election-day **Ocoee Massacre**. When Black citizens of Ocoee tried to vote, brutal mob violence ensued. At least 30 Black people were murdered, and hundreds were driven from their homes and out of the city, making Ocoee an all-white town. No one was ever held responsible for the death and destruction; local and federal authorities declined to investigate.

In the annals of injustice, the case of the **Groveland Four** stands out. In 1949, four young, local African American men were falsely accused of rape by a white woman from Groveland; two of the accused were murdered (one by a posse, the other by notorious Sheriff Willis McCall while in his custody); one received the death sentence (later commuted); and the fourth, a 16-year-old, was sentenced to life in prison. The State of Florida officially pardoned all four men in 2019 posthumously, 70 years after the Groveland events. For a thorough and compelling account of the Groveland Four, read Gilbert King's Pulitzer Prize–winning nonfiction book *Devil in the Grove*.

throughout the region, particularly if you travel away from the C2C. Fortunately, the trail itself preserves an unhurried version of the area, one that respects nature and protects history. The value of shared-use recreational paths is enthusiastically recognized by many residents not just as a neighborhood amenity but also as a significant economic, health, and lifestyle benefit.

TRAIL SECTION 5
CLERMONT TO SPRING HILL

LAKE, SUMTER, AND HERNANDO COUNTIES, INCLUDING THE TOWNS OF CLERMONT, WEBSTER, AND BROOKSVILLE

Trail section length: 55 miles
Point A: Clermont Waterfront Park, 330 Third Street, Clermont
Point B: Suncoast Parkway/SR 50 Trailhead, Spring Hill, at the southwest corner of the intersection of the Suncoast Parkway/SR 589 and SR 50
Optional spur trails: Withlacoochee Trail and Van Fleet Trail

HIGHLIGHTS
Lake Hiawatha Preserve
Scenic Withlacoochee and Good Neighbor Trails
Croom Wildlife Management Area
Historic Brooksville

TRAILHEADS
Clermont Waterfront Park, 330 Third St., Clermont
Lake Hiawatha Preserve, 450 12th St., Clermont
Withlacoochee Trailhead, intersection of Croom Rital Road and SR 50
(continued below)

Trail Section 5—Clermont to Spring Hill Trailhead

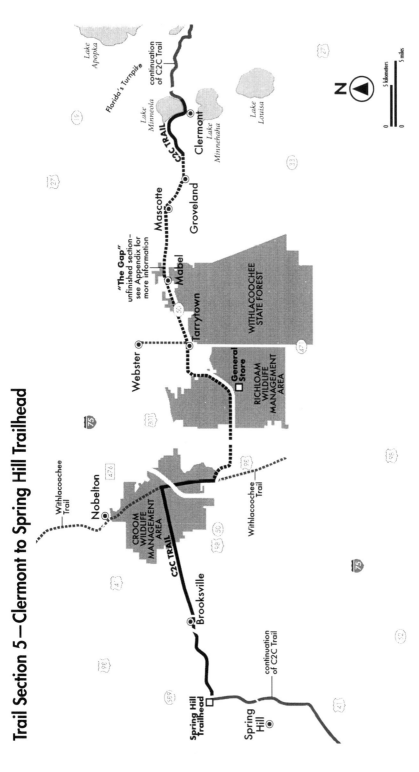

Trail Section 5: Clermont to Spring Hill Trailhead. At the time of publication, there is a 28-mile incomplete gap of the C2C between Groveland and the Withlacoochee Trail. Riding on SR 50 is not advisable. See Appendix for information about crossing this gap.

TRAILHEADS (*continued*)

Croom MTB Parking 1, 11281 Croom Rital Rd., Brooksville,
    one mile north of the C2C via the Withlacoochee Trail
Russell Street Park, 70 Russell St., Brooksville
Suncoast Trail SR 50 Trailhead, southwest corner of the intersec-
    tion of the Suncoast Parkway SR 589 and SR 50, Springhill

For information about Clermont, see Trail Section 4.

THE ROUTE: NEED TO KNOW

At the time of publication, this section contains the **longest gap** of
the trail, approximately 28 miles in a direct route. While a completion deadline is not yet available, it is unlikely to be finished before
2025. Many cyclists have found other informal routes, all of which
include riding on roads. Because these are alternate routes and use
existing roads, they are also **longer mileage** than the anticipated
completed trail route. Specifically, the gap is between Groveland and the Withlacoochee Trail. In Groveland, the C2C Trail
abruptly ends just north of the intersection of CR 565A and SR
50. At the Withlacoochee Trail, the C2C ends at the Croom Rital
Road Trailhead, at the intersection of the Withlacoochee Trail and
SR 50. Note that in this area, SR 50 is also called Cortez Boulevard. **For unofficial routes** that cross the gap, see "**Appendix:
Crossing the Gap between Groveland and Brooksville.**"

C2C travelers are creative in finding other ways to cross the
gap. Some use automobile support by having a friend or family
member drive them across. Others have hired drivers; possibilities
include Lyft or Uber using their "XL" option to request a large
vehicle. Car or van rental is also a possibility, and both Clermont
and Brooksville have car rental locations. Segment riders can simply put the gap at the beginning and end of segment rides.

The C2C across this gap is in varying stages of completion.
In some areas, construction has already begun, but other areas
lag behind. For updates, go to https://floridadep.gov/parks/ogt/
content/florida-coast-coast-trail, and click on the link to the status
map.

Trail Section 5 of the C2C uses portions of several regional trails: South Lake Trail, Withlacoochee Trail, Good Neighbor Trail, and the Good Neighbor Connector. When construction is finished, the yet unnamed SR 50 Sumter/Lake County trail will complete this section.

Make note of the **intersection of the Suncoast Trail** and **Cortez Boulevard/SR 50 Trail**. The connection between these two paths is at the southwest corner of the intersection of the Suncoast Parkway and SR 50. The Suncoast Trail continues northward 11 miles toward the town of Homosassa. This northern section is not part of the C2C Trail.

Camping is available at Silver Lake Campground in the Croom Wildlife Management Area. Hog Island Recreation Area and Campground, slightly off the C2C route, is accessible by bicycle via Nobleton CR 476.

RECOMMENDED WALKS

Between **Clermont Waterfront Park** (330 Third St.) and **Lake Hiawatha Preserve** (450 12th St.), walkers enjoy two miles of lakeshore views from the C2C Trail. Parking is available at both ends, as are water fountains and restrooms. The lake often brings cooling breezes to the trail, and the recreational opportunities of the area attract plenty of visitors. Along the way, wander through the **Clermont Historic Village Museum** (490 West Ave.) to see artifacts of bygone times as well as historic homes, a schoolhouse, and a train depot. Head into the small downtown of Clermont, two blocks south of the trail, for food and drinks.

A quiet walk from the center of **Brooksville** starts at the **Russell Street Park**. Head east on this C2C section of the Good Neighbor Trail. In 10 miles, the trail reaches the paved Withlacoochee Trail. The path is remote and offers a nice escape from cars and commercial development. The trail has both sunny and shady sections; bring plenty of water, as there are no facilities.

The trail along Lake Minneola by Clermont

LOCAL CULTURE

This mainly rural part of Florida offers glimpses of small-town life, pastureland, and preserved natural terrain. Between Clermont and Brooksville, towns are sparse. Groveland and Mascotte have commercial business near the C2C but have not yet developed inviting town centers. As a result, much of this short five-mile section includes uninspired surroundings. The long 24-mile stretch between Mascotte and the Withlacoochee Trailhead passes through the Richloam Wildlife Management Area. Just east of Brooksville, the C2C cuts through another remote area, the Croom Wildlife Management Area.

In the early 1900s, major local industries were agriculture, rock mining, timber, and turpentine production. Even today, the small towns along the C2C route reflect this economic past.

The **Lake County Citrus Label Tour**, organized by the Lake County Historical Society, pays tribute to the citrus industry and its importance both as an economic driver and in creating agriculturally based communities. The tour includes three towns on the C2C: Clermont, Groveland, and Mascotte. Growers of the mid-1900s took pride in their crops and created unique and colorful crate labels to advertise and promote their oranges and grapefruits. Growers hoped that the visibility of their brand would increase demand for their fruit. These lithograph labels began to fall out of use in the 1950s when cardboard packing boxes started to replace wooden crates. Vintage labels have since become collectible works of art due to their iconic style. Stop to see the signs, take a photo, and recall the glory days of Central Florida citrus. Visit these Label Tour locations near the C2C:

Clermont Historical Village (490 West Ave., Clermont)

Groveland Museum (243 S. Lake Ave., Groveland)

Mascotte Civic Center (121 N. Sunset Ave., Mascotte)

For more information on this Citrus Label Tour and the history of citrus in Lake County, see https://www.historyoflake countycitrus.com.

A four-mile spur trail, heading north from Tarrytown to Webster, leads to **Swap-O-Rama Webster Westside Flea Market** (516 NW Third St., Webster) held every Monday, rain or shine. This huge, bustling flea market attracts buyers from across the state. Shoppers will find antiques and collectibles as well as furniture, electronics, clothing, tools, and jewelry. Vendors also sell food and drinks. Unlike the Monday-only flea market, the **Farmer's Market Restaurant** is open for breakfast and lunch every day.

The notable **Richloam General Store** and historic post office (38219 Richloam Clay Sink Rd., Webster) is located 0.7 mile south of the C2C. This tiny, charming store was built in 1928 to serve the local community (including nearby turpentine camps) and the railroad station. Rocking chairs set out in front invite you to sit and relax, and the store stocks a variety of goods that harken back to the 1920s: candy, sodas, dry goods, jams, jellies, sauces, and aprons. It is listed on the National Register of Historic Places and is the sole remaining building from the early Richloam community. To get here, turn south from the C2C on Porter Gap Road. The name of this unpaved road changes to Richloam Clay Sink Road. Although the road is unpaved, its firm-packed, crushed-lime-rock surface is easy to ride.

The Richloam General Store captures the atmosphere of bygone days.

Brooksville's historic train depot

Brooksville's cultural sites chronicle the stories of its past, both good and bad. The original **1885 Train Depot** (70 Russell St.) is adjacent to the C2C at Russell Street Park, a C2C trailhead. This depot served the former railroad that ran through Brooksville; the track heading east from town is now the C2C/Good Neighbor Trail. The depot, with its restored interior and objects from its era as a working train station, focuses on the role that railroads played in the settlement of Brooksville. Explore the inside of a restored boxcar that transported lumber workers into the Green Swamp to harvest cypress trees.

School days of the past are re-created in the **Countryman One Room Schoolhouse** (66 Russell St.), situated next to the train depot. It is a rather nondescript building from the outside and was built in 2014 in the style of the first schoolhouse in Hernando County, which was erected in 1852. Original wooden school desks and interactive lessons allow visitors to re-create the feeling of pioneer-era schooling.

For an elegant look into Brooksville's past, visit the **Hernando Heritage Museum** in the **May-Stringer House** (601 Museum Ct.). The genteel four-story, gabled Victorian home with ginger-bread trim displays historical artifacts in Victorian-style rooms.

The museum is less than one mile north of the C2C in downtown Brooksville, and the detour to the museum gives you the opportunity to wander through town. On Friday and Saturday nights, partake in the museum's ghost tours (book in advance, for a fee).

Weeki Wachee Springs State Park is six miles west of the C2C's Suncoast Parkway/SR 50 Trailhead. This park was made famous by its underwater "mermaid" show, which originated in 1947. The mermaids are women dressed in costumes who swim and perform in the crystal-clear spring water while breathing oxygen supplied through hoses. Viewers sit in a submerged amphitheater dug into lime rock and view the show through wide windows. Originally a privately owned enterprise, the State of Florida bought the property for a state park in 2008 and continued the historic mermaid show. To get to Weeki Wachee Springs, use the bicycle lanes or sidewalks along SR 50, although the cycling conditions are not ideal due to the high volume of automobile traffic.

NATURE

Just west of the Clermont Waterfront Park area is picturesque **Lake Hiawatha Preserve** (450 12th St., Clermont). This preserve is an expansive 220-acre park that includes playgrounds, picnic areas, a pavilion, dog parks, walking paths, restrooms, and a highly rated disc golf course. The large, well-designed playground has a replica water tower, including a water spigot that splashes water for fun or to cool off. Stop here to enjoy the shade of stately Live Oak trees and the breeze from Lake Minneola.

These **Live Oak trees** (*Quercus virginiana*) are perhaps the most majestic of the many different species of oak trees that are native to Florida. Live Oaks grow in a wide range of habitats throughout the state, including upland woods, coastal hammocks, and suburban landscapes. These trees can be enormous, growing up to 60 feet tall, and often spread out much wider than their height. You can identify this tree by its wide-spreading growth habit, sometimes with low, curving branches, and its deeply grooved bark. In Florida, these trees are never bare; they lose their

Spanish Moss (*Tillandsia usneoides*)

Throughout Central Florida, Spanish Moss hangs from the branches of Live Oak trees and sways gracefully in the breeze. Contrary to its name, Spanish Moss is not a true moss, nor is it native to Spain. The plant is in the bromeliad family. Unlike parasitic plants such as mistletoe, Spanish Moss does not harm trees by taking nutrients from them; instead, it gets its nourishment and water from the air and rain.

Spanish Moss was once used for blankets, string, insulation, and furniture stuffing until it was replaced by modern synthetic materials. Early citrus growers wadded it into wooden barrels with oranges to protect the fruit during shipping. Small birds can often be seen foraging for insects in the moss, and some use it for nest material.

leaves in spring only when new leaves are ready to emerge. Spanish Moss and resurrection fern often flourish on Live Oak trees.

Between Tarrytown and the Withlacoochee Trail, the C2C crosses the **Richloam Wildlife Management Area**, part of the Withlacoochee State Forest. If you want to enter deep into this tract, you can access it directly from SR 50 at Porter Gap Road. It is an interesting place to explore. Wild turkey, deer, birds, and reptiles make this habitat home. While some roads are suitable for gravel/touring bicycles, others are better suited for mountain bikes. This area is not maintained as a recreational park, so be prepared for the wilderness and perhaps obstacles. A few of the unpaved roads may have standing water or soft sand. Limited hunting is permitted in the Wildlife Management Area according to a specific schedule (see https://www.fdacs.gov/Forest-Wildfire/Our-Forests/State-Forests/Withlacoochee-State-Forest).

The **Croom Wildlife Management Area**, 7 miles northeast of Brooksville and approximately 10 miles west of Webster, covers

20,000 acres of preserved land, most of which is longleaf pine habitat. The management area allows for a variety of recreational uses, including hiking, hunting, fishing, wildlife viewing, primitive camping, horseback riding, and off-road bicycling. The Good Neighbor Trail portion of the C2C crosses through a section of Croom.

While traveling Section 5, you'll cross the **Brooksville Ridge**, a 100-mile north-south ridge of land. The highest point in Brooksville is 190 feet (60 meters) above sea level; heading both east and west from town are gently rolling hills as the elevation quickly drops to approximately 30 feet (9 meters). To the west of Brooksville are coastal lowlands of the Gulf of Mexico, while to the east is the Withlacoochee River and its large basin of freshwater wetlands. The Brooksville Ridge runs parallel to the larger Lake Wales Ridge, which lies 40 miles to the east (see Trail Section 4). Longleaf pine and turkey oak trees are common in this dry, sandy ridge ecosystem.

The **geologically accessible limestone** in Sumter and Hernando Counties have made this area conducive to limestone quarries. Much of this limestone, part of the Ocala Limestone Formation, is at or near the earth's surface. Because limestone is a permeable sedimentary rock, rainwater can seep through it down into Florida's aquifer, thus making this area important to the state's water supply. Limestone is also prized as a road and building material, and limestone quarries have operated in Florida since the days of the first European settlers. While they are economically important to the area, they are not without critics due to environmental degradation issues related to air quality, habitat destruction, and the blighted pits that remain when mining operations cease. The **Brooksville Quarry Disc Golf Course** (800 John Gary Grubbs Blvd.), close to the center of town, was built on a former limestone quarry. Now planted with grass and trees, the course offers disc golfers the chance to enjoy changes in elevation caused by former mining operations. Visit this course and see the former quarry, accessible by bicycle from Tom Varn Park (301 Darby Ln.).

Directly along the C2C, a **limestone quarry** operates on the northeast corner of SR 50 and US 301. The quarry is barely visible from the road; you'll see only a sign and truck traffic. Limestone has a wide range of uses. Quarried limestone can be used as a building material, but perhaps more importantly, today, powdered limestone is used in cement making. Crushed limestone is often employed in the building of roads and highways, for which there is tremendous demand in Florida. The agricultural industry also uses limestone as an additive to soils to adjust acidity levels and provide calcium to plants. From an aerial view, the ponds at the quarries have an amazing light blue color due to the presence in the water of finely powered limestone rock. For over a century, rock mining and cement making have been important sources of economic growth and employment for this area.

HISTORICAL NOTES

Spanish explorers who traveled through this section of western Florida in the 15th and 16th centuries seldom made permanent settlements. Most of this area was occupied by Florida's indigenous people until migrants of European descent moved here in the early 1800s. By that time, Florida was the home of the Seminole Tribe. Members of the Seminoles come from a variety of indigenous groups, some of whom had fled to Florida to escape clashes with Europeans in the north. Conflicts ensued when land inhabited by the Seminoles was claimed and settled by these new immigrants. As US soldiers were deployed to secure land and to protect settlers, they created economic incentives for additional settlers because the army needed roads, supplies, and services. Hostilities and violence between the warring parties occurred from 1817 to 1858; by the end of that time, most of the native Seminoles had been killed or driven from the state. Many were forced to move to what is currently the State of Oklahoma, although a small number were able to survive in remote southern parts of Florida.

The **Dade Battlefield**, which is now a park that commemorates one of conflicts of the Seminole Wars, is 11 miles north of the C2C. On December 28, 1835, native Seminoles attacked US soldiers who were marching to Tampa Bay to reinforce a fort. The commander, Major Francis Dade, was killed immediately. By the end of the day, 108 soldiers were dead, while only three escaped. The event became known as the "Dade Massacre." Seminole tribesmen deaths and injuries are unknown. The event was the ignition point for further escalation of the clashes throughout the state. **Dade Battlefield Historic State Park** (7200 Battlefield Pkwy., Bushnell) provides visitors with the opportunity to understand the hostilities at the center of the Seminole Wars. Additionally, the park has picnic pavilions and hiking trails, and its natural setting offers the chance to see wildlife.

In this trail section, the C2C passes through territory that owes much of its early industry to the introduction of the railroad. Rail connections provided agricultural, timber, turpentine, and mining operations with the means of transporting their resources to markets. Many of the small communities that grew up around these enterprises have disappeared. Some, like the unincorporated town of **Mabel**, are still listed on maps but have few inhabitants. Mabel once served as the junction of two railway lines and was large enough to warrant a post office (it was named for the postmaster's daughter) and had a thriving sawmill. Eventually most of the town's residents moved to Linden, a slightly larger town nearby. The post office closed in 1918, and little has changed since.

Tarrytown is an unincorporated area of Sumter County and today consists mostly of an intersection with a convenience store and gas stations. On the southwest corner of this intersection is the Robbins Manufacturing Company. The company was founded in 1938 as an industrial sawmill, a reflection of the economic importance of the lumber business in Florida at the time. The company currently operates the largest wood-products facility in the state and manufactures heavy-duty items from wood such as utility poles and marine pilings as well as fence posts. Although its headquarters are in Tampa, the company's lumber mill still operates in Tarrytown.

Turpentine Camps

Florida's natural pine forests were ideal places to extract and process turpentine. To extract the resin, the trees were tapped with a sharp implement, and gummy sap was collected into cups as it oozed from the wood. At first, turpentine was primarily used for waterproofing the seams between beams on ship hulls and for preserving ropes. Later, it was used in paints, varnishes, oils, and even home products such as soap and ointments. Longleaf pine forests, preferred for turpentine, once covered a huge swath of land in the southeastern United States. Today, it is estimated that only 3 percent of this once-expansive longleaf pine ecosystem remains.

The turpentine businesses in the United States began in the mid-Atlantic region but slowly moved southward from Virginia as pine forests were razed. In Florida, the industry flourished in the mid-1800s, and by the early 1900s the sale of turpentine was Florida's second largest industry; only citrus was larger. Rough conditions and brutal treatment of turpentine workers meant that these camps had few voluntary employees. Turpentine camps often used prison labor, and most of these laborers were Black. In 1924, Florida's legislature ended the practice of leasing convicts to private industries.

By the 1920s, many of Florida's turpentine camps converted to timber mills or disbanded as turpentine production waned (today Brazil is the top turpentine producer and exporter). Most turpentine camps fell to ruin, and traces of them have disappeared. The Etna Turpentine Camp near Inverness (a town along the Withlacoochee State Trail) was uncovered in the 1990s, nearly a century after the camp's demise, when a gas pipeline route was being studied. This archeological find is a reminder of the hardscrabble days of turpentine production.

If you are in search of a ghost town, visit the abandoned town of **Croom**, on the C2C near the intersection of the Withlacoochee Trail and the Good Neighbor Trail. This village was yet another of many along the C2C that owed its birth to the 19th-century railways. In addition to a rail station, Croom had the advantage of being close to a small ferry—and later a bridge—that crossed the Withlacoochee River. But Croom was deserted long ago, and you must look intently for evidence of its existence. Search among the overgrowth for foundations of buildings, pieces of metal rail tracks, broken ceramics, traces of former roads, and the remains of the bridge across the Withlacoochee River. Note that archeological sites are protected and nothing may be removed, damaged, or disturbed.

The settler's town of **Brooksville** was first preceded by a fort built to protect settlers from the indigenous tribes. Among the

The Hernando County Courthouse, built in 1913, located in the center of Brooksville. Picnic tables in front of the courthouse are ideal for a lunch stop.

pioneering families who moved here in the 1840s were citrus growers, bankers, merchants, and plantation owners. The settlement's prosperity led to its formal establishment as a town in 1856. A large and imposing courthouse in the center of Brooksville (20 N. Main St.) is one indication of its early regional importance as the governmental center of Hernando County. The architect of this courthouse, William A. Edwards, was also the architect of most of the original buildings on the University of Florida campus in Gainesville.

Brooksville's name is a source of modern-day reflection and sometimes controversy. The town's name was chosen in honor of the now-infamous congressman from South Carolina, Preston Brooks, who viciously assaulted and seriously injured US Senator Charles Sumner in 1856. The assault occurred in the US Senate Chamber after Sumner gave an impassioned antislavery speech. Upon the incorporation of the town that same year, its citizens chose the name Brooksville in honor of Preston Brooks, the violent supporter of slavery.

The **Spring Hill African American Cemetery** (8580 Fort Dade Ave., Brooksville) is just 1.5 miles north of the C2C. This historic cemetery dates to the 1850s, before the Civil War, and is the resting place of many of Brooksville's slaves and Black residents. The heavily wooded area is accessible by an unpaved road. Brooksville's wealth in the mid-1800s was partially due to the slave labor used by white landowners.

For an in-depth look at Brooksville, including many historical photographs, I recommend two books: *Images of America: Brooksville* by Robert Martinez and *Hernando County, Florida, Black America Series* by Imani D. Asukile.

OPTIONAL SPUR TRAIL: WITHLACOOCHEE STATE TRAIL

The Withlacoochee State Trail, a pleasant and interesting path, is 46 miles long, from Trilby at the south end to Citrus Springs at the north end. The C2C path travels on the Withlacoochee

Trail for 4.5 miles, from the Good Neighbor Trail intersection (11 miles east of Brooksville) to the Croom Rital Road/SR 50 Trailhead. The Withlacoochee Trail was originally a railroad line established in the late 1800s, but after it fell into disuse, the State of Florida purchased the property in 1989 to create this scenic recreational trail. Trail users can venture south along the Withlacoochee Trail to the tiny hamlet of Trilby or head north to Citrus Springs. The towns of Floral City and Inverness, as well as Fort Cooper State Park, are highlights of the northern section. This trail is typically shady and picturesque and is a favorite of local bicyclists.

OPTIONAL SPUR TRAIL: VAN FLEET TRAIL

If you like a long, flat, straight course, this is the trail for you. Over 29 miles long, the Van Fleet Trail has just one curve. It crosses through isolated territory, situated in the undeveloped area of the **Green Swamp**. The secluded nature of the Van Fleet Trail leads to some interesting wildlife-viewing opportunities, particularly in early morning or evening. Common sightings include turkeys, alligators, white-tailed deer, fox squirrels, snakes, and a variety of birds.

The Green Swamp comprises wetlands, flatlands, and sandy ridges. While a portion of the rainwater that falls on the Green Swamp drains across the earth's surface, some of it seeps down into the aquifer (see box below). The water that remains on the surface flows down from the swamp's slightly elevated setting and creates four separate, significant rivers (the Hillsborough, Withlacoochee, Ocklawaha, and Peace). The protection of the Green Swamp is important to safeguard Florida's water quality, preserve habitat for wildlife, and provide recreational opportunities.

The Green Swamp and Florida's Aquifer

Most of Florida's drinking water comes from its aquifer, a huge system of porous rocks through which water moves. Most of this porous rock is made of limestone, sand, and shells. Because of both its size and its geology, the Green Swamp is an indispensable recharge area for Florida's aquifer. Across the approximately 875 square miles of the Green Swamp, rainwater can seep through the earth's surface and filter down into the aquifer.

Over half of Florida's water supply is pumped out from the aquifer, and in Central and North Florida the aquifer satisfies nearly 90 percent of water demand. The health of the Green Swamp is an important piece of the process that ensures clean water for Floridians and visitors. Conserving water and eliminating pollutants are also integral to the security of the water supply.

Most of the Green Swamp's acreage is located south of the C2C Trail through Sumter and Hernando Counties. The portion of the C2C along SR 50 between Tarrytown and US 301 passes through the swamp. Be sure to stop along the swamp to admire its beauty and appreciate its significance.

TRAIL SECTION 6
SPRING HILL TO TARPON SPRINGS

HERNANDO, PASCO, AND PINELLAS COUNTIES

Trail section length: 47 miles

Point A: Suncoast/SR 50 Trailhead, Spring Hill, at the intersection of the Suncoast Parkway/SR 589 and SR 50

Point B: 10 S. Safford Ave., Tarpon Springs

For information on Tarpon Springs, see Trail Section 7.

HIGHLIGHTS
Jay B. Starkey Wilderness Park
Brooker Creek Preserve and Environmental Education Center
Miles of uninterrupted riding

TRAILHEADS
Suncoast Trail State Road 50 Trailhead, southwest corner of the
    Suncoast Parkway/SR 589 and SR 50 intersection, Springhill
Anderson Snow Park, 1360 Anderson Snow Rd., Springhill
Jay B. Starkey Wilderness Park, 10500 Wilderness Park Blvd.,
    New Port Richey

(*continued below*)

Trail Section 6 — Spring Hill Trailhead to Tarpon Springs

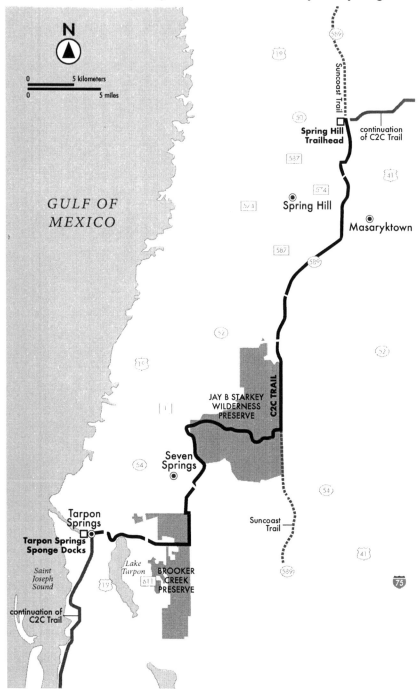

TRAILHEADS (*continued*)
Starkey Park Bike Trailhead, 11115 Wilderness Park Blvd., New
   Port Richey
Brooker Creek Preserve, 3940 Keystone Rd., Tarpon Springs

THE ROUTE: NEED TO KNOW
This segment of the C2C connects four local trails: the Suncoast
Trail, the Starkey Wilderness Park Trail, the Starkey Boulevard
Trail, and the Tri-County Trail. The Suncoast Trail provides 23
miles of almost uninterrupted cycling. Along these 23 miles, there
are few facilities for water or refreshments, so be prepared for
exposure to the elements and bring plenty of water, sunscreen, and
snacks. The Starkey Wilderness Park Trail is a scenic path and has
facilities such as restrooms and water fountains.

Note the **intersection of the Suncoast Trail and Starkey
Wilderness Trail**. If you are heading **west on the C2C** route (and
therefore, south on the Suncoast Trail), the C2C departs from
the Suncoast Trail and makes a 90-degree turn onto the Starkey
Wilderness Park Bike Trail approximately 5.5 miles south of SR
52. The Suncoast Trail continues farther south from this point, so
you'll need to look for this intersection. If you are heading **east on
the C2C**, you'll follow the Starkey Wilderness Bike Trail until its
eastern end at the Suncoast Trail, at which point you'll turn left
(north) to stay on the C2C route.

There is potentially confusing signage at the **intersection of
Keystone Road and East Lake Road**. The C2C Trail parallels
Keystone Road in Pinellas County for just over five miles. At the
intersection of Keystone Road and East Lake Road (four miles east
of the city of Tarpon Springs), the signage may be misleading. Do
not turn south onto the trail parallel to East Lake Road; stay on the
Keystone Road path. The East Lake Road Trail is currently a spur
path and is not part of the C2C (although there are long-range
plans to incorporate it into the Pinellas County loop trail system).

Camping is available at Jay B. Starkey Wilderness Park.

RECOMMENDED WALKS

The most picturesque and rewarding walks along this segment of the C2C incorporate two large nature preserves: Brooker Creek Preserve and Jay B. Starkey Wilderness Park.

The **Brooker Creek Preserve** (3940 Keystone Rd., Tarpon Springs) is a beautiful, forested area (see "Nature" section below). The well-signed entrance to the preserve is directly on the C2C along Keystone Road. Car parking and the education center are located one mile south of the entrance. From there, choose between four loop trails, the 0.7-mile Education Center Trail, the 1.5-mile Flatwoods Trail, the 2.8-mile Blackwater Cutoff Trail, or the 4-mile Wilderness Trail (trail mileages listed here are the total mileage for each loop). Note that the longer trails may include wet paths and shallow water crossings and the conditions will vary based on the season and recent rainfall. Excellent trail maps are available on premises and can also be found on the Preserve's website: http://www.brookercreekpreserve.org.

Farther north, the C2C route passes through the heart of the **Jay B. Starkey Wilderness Park** (10500 Wilderness Park Blvd.), which is a superb place for walkers and hikers. Stay on the C2C to explore 7 miles of this park, or take advantage of the additional 13 miles of unpaved trails. The paved and unpaved paths can be combined in a variety of ways, taking hikers through a range of habitats. These options allow you to choose between the busier asphalt paths or quieter unpaved trails. For more information about the park, see the "Nature" section below.

The Suncoast Trail section of the C2C, running between SR 50 and Jay B. Starkey Wilderness Park, is predominantly a straight path parallel to the Suncoast Parkway with few facilities or trailheads. Along this section, there are limited points of interest, but the allure of an uninterrupted trail may be inviting to long-distance walkers and runners.

Cypress and pine trees border a shallow lake in the Jay B. Starkey Wilderness Park.

LOCAL CULTURE

In this section, the C2C route crosses remote terrain with few towns or landmarks. Along the Suncoast Parkway between SR 50 and SR 52, the trail passes by modern subdivisions of homes to the west and rural pastures to the east. Most of the populated towns of this area lie 10 miles west of the C2C along the Gulf Coast or 20 miles inland eastward near Dade City. As a result, the culture of Pasco County is difficult to experience while on the C2C unless you make plans to venture off the trail. However, you can explore the natural environment by spending time at Brooker Creek Preserve and the Jay B. Starkey Wilderness Park, both of which are extraordinary (see "Nature" below).

For an intriguing story of immigration, visit the tiny town of **Masaryktown**. Masaryktown is just 1.5 miles from the C2C, due east of the intersection of the C2C and County Line Road (SR 578). A Slovak-language newspaper editor in New York City created the town in 1924 to offer fellow immigrants a better life than working factory jobs. He purchased land and formed a corporation, then sold acreage to founding shareholders intending to plant and grow orange trees. The town's name honors the first president of the then–newly created Czechoslovakia, Tomáš Masaryk. Citrus trees were planted by the original 61 Slovak and Czech settlers. But the trees did not survive, and the families turned to poultry farming and canning. Although few descendants (if any) of the original immigrants live here now, vestiges of their early settlement remain in the names of streets, many of which are named after prominent Czech and Slovak individuals.

NATURE

As a respite from the sunny section of the C2C along the Suncoast Parkway, take a short excursion to **Crews Lake Wilderness Park** (16739 Crews Lake Dr., Spring Hill), just over one mile from the C2C via quiet roads. Head east at the intersection of the C2C and Caldwell Lane, cross over the Suncoast Parkway on a low-traffic road with a wide shoulder, then turn right (south) on Lenway Road for about one mile until you reach Crews Lake Drive. This 113-acre rustic county park offers hiking trails, picnic facilities, play areas, primitive camping, and a railway museum, including an operational small-scale replica train. Climb the observation tower overlooking the lake and wetlands, or walk the boardwalk for close views of nature. The lake level has declined since 2000, reportedly due to the demand for water for nearby subdivisions. The park's bird checklist includes over 160 species of birds that have been sighted here. Walk through the park for a representative sampling of Florida habitats, including oak hammocks, scrubby flatwoods, sandhills, and cypress domes. In addition to birds, this park is home to alligators, racoons, squirrels, and several species of butterflies.

Florida's Palm "Trees"

The palm tree is an iconic symbol of Florida. There's something about graceful fronds rustling in the breeze that evokes relaxation. Palms are easy to recognize by their single, unbranched trunks and their unusual large leaves, called fronds. Florida's official state tree is the common Sabal Palm (*Sabal palmetto*), which grows in a variety of habitats throughout the state. The berries of Sabal Palms provide food for wildlife, while the old leaf stalks provide a habitat for small animals.

Palms are not true trees; they are monocots, which are genetically more closely related to grasses and orchids than they are to trees. Palms lack the outer bark/inner wood structure of true trees. Instead, with palms and all monocots, the entire trunk contains living tissue.

While only 12 palm species are considered native to Florida, over 30 different species grow here, many of which were introduced from South America or Asia. Look closely to notice the many different sizes and shapes of the fronds as well as the texture of the trunks.

Florida's palms are usually planted for their landscape value, but some produce edible fruit (e.g., coconuts); others have an edible small core known as "heart of palm"; and some yield palm oil. Palms were used by Indigenous people and early settlers for building materials, and fronds were often used as thatch for roofing shelter. Additionally, fibrous strands from the leaves can be twisted together, a convenient way to form rope.

Sabal Palms, often called Cabbage Palms, are Florida's state tree.

Seven miles east of Tarpon Springs is the exceptional **Brooker Creek Preserve and Environmental Education Center** (3940 Keystone Rd.). The C2C Trail borders the northern end of the preserve. There is excellent signage, so it is easy to find. The Education Center building and hiking paths are located about one mile south from the entrance on Keystone Road. This 8,700-acre preserve is the largest preserved natural area in Pinellas County. It is operated by the county government and free to the public.

The **Brooker Creek Preserve** encompasses a variety of natural habitats, such as forested wetlands, oak hammocks, cypress domes, and pine flatwoods. The preserve was established as a wildlife refuge and to protect the quality of the region's water. Much of the water from the preserve flows south to Lake Tarpon and Tampa Bay. There are several excellent hiking trails, ranging from a short 0.7-mile trail near the Education Center to a more strenuous 4-mile hike that passes through the wide variety of ecosystems of the area (note that parts of this trail may be wet). For birders, a separate short path near the Preserve's Education Center ends at a viewing blind alongside a freshwater marsh with the chance to see wading and migratory birds. The Education Center is well worth visiting. There you will find exhibits about Florida's ecosystems, classrooms, restrooms, and a small gift shop. Stop in to purchase snacks, drinks, books, or even native plants from the nursery.

Florida is subject to huge thunderstorms, bringing lightning along with rain, and lightning causes **wildfires**. With the settlement of the state, wildfires were suppressed for decades by humans hoping to protect land and property. Floridians have since come to understand the value of periodic fires, and the Brooker Creek Preserve, like many preserved lands in Florida, has instituted a prescribed fire program.

Prescribed fires reduce the amount of potential fuel for fires, thereby limiting the chances of a large, uncontrollable blaze, while also providing benefits to the natural habitat, such as disease control. We now know that some plants and animals rely on periodic fires for their survival. For example, some pinecones require fire to reproduce. The fire's heat melts the resins in the pinecone, which allows them to open and disperse their seeds. Gopher tortoises and Red-cockaded Woodpeckers also rely on periodic fires to maintain the habitat crucial for their survival.

Jay B. Starkey Wilderness Park (10500 Wilderness Park Blvd., New Port Richey) has 8,300 acres of natural public lands, including trails for bicyclists, equestrians, and hikers; covered pavilions; and a playground. In addition to the 7 miles of paved bicycling trails that are on the C2C path, the park has over 13 additional miles of unpaved hiking trails. The Starkey Wilderness is recognized as one of the most significant conservation areas in the Tampa Bay region due to its size and biological diversity.

Longleaf pine flatwoods, cypress swamps, sand pine scrub, and oak forests can all be found here. The Starkey Environmental Education Center is used for environmental programs relating to the park's ecosystems. Take a short amble starting at the Corral Parking Lot on Wilderness Park Boulevard and head east on the

Jay B. Starkey Park provides excellent opportunities to enjoy Florida's natural environment.

Gopher Tortoises

The gopher tortoise (*Gopherus polyphemus*) is designated by the State of Florida as a threatened species, its population decline primarily due to loss of its habitat. These long-lived reptiles are approximately 10 inches long when fully grown. In the wild, a gopher tortoise typically lives 40 to 60 years, and in captivity, they can live more than 90 years according to the Florida Fish and Wildlife Conservation Commission.

Gopher tortoises prefer sandy soils, where they can dig long burrows. The burrows provide a stable environment that shields them from extreme temperatures but also allows them to escape from predators. Scientists estimate that over 200 other species are dependent on the tortoises' burrows, often making use of a burrow after it is abandoned by the tortoise.

The dry, sandy land that gopher tortoises favor is also sought after by humans for residential and commercial building. This land-use conflict is the main source of tortoise habitat loss in Florida.

Look for these nearly foot-long reptiles all along the C2C path but particularly in arid, sandy locations. They are generally slow moving and scare easily, retreating into their shell or burrow if they feel vulnerable.

Gopher tortoises (*Gopherus polyphemus*) can be found in dry, sandy areas of central Florida.

wooded path to the Grassy Lake Bird Blind. The bird blind, constructed by the West Pasco Audubon Society, is just 100 yards from the parking lot. This shallow lake is habitat to many species, and the blind provides an excellent wildlife viewing opportunity.

Campsites are also available (use the park's online reservations system). For more information, see https://www.pascocountyfl.net/304/Jay-B-Starkey-Wilderness-Park.

The north section of the Jay B. Starkey Wilderness Park is the preserve's more remote **Serenova Tract** (14900 SR 52, Land O' Lakes), managed by the Southwest Florida Water Management District. The tract was placed under the protection of the Water Management District to mitigate wetland destruction that occurred during the construction of the Suncoast Parkway. Access the Serenova Tract from the C2C by traveling one mile west on SR 52 via a shared-use path. Over 6,000 acres of natural land await visitors who can explore on 20 miles of hiking, bicycling, and equestrian trails. Fishing and camping are also permitted here. This tract supports wildlife such as wild turkeys, white-tailed deer, gopher tortoises, armadillos, and possums. Feral hogs also roam the area; give them wide berth if you see any. Hogs leave unmistakable evidence of their disruptive presence, sometimes creating shallow craters when they dig up soil and trample an area.

Jay B. Starkey Wilderness Preserve and the Serenova Tract are important protectors of the watershed for both the Anclote and Pithlachascotee Rivers, both of which flow southwest from the preserved area in meandering paths toward the Gulf of Mexico. The Anclote River passes directly by the historic sponge docks of Tarpon Springs (see Trail Section 7), while the Pithlachascotee ends its trek at the Gulf of Mexico near Port Richey.

As the C2C travels parallel to Starkey Boulevard, it passes by **Heartwood Preserve** (4100 Starkey Blvd., Trinity). This preserve is unique; it is a privately owned natural burial property, designed to provide a place where loved ones can be buried in conservation land using environmentally sensitive practices. Heartwood Preserve is located on longleaf pine flatwood habitat and cypress wetlands, both of which can be seen from the C2C, and provides a biological buffer for the Anclote River. The founder of Heartwood Preserve descends from the Starkey family. A longtime pioneering cattle-ranching family of the area, the Starkey family donated land to help establish the Jay B. Starkey Wilderness Park and Preserve.

The geology in Pasco County is conducive to the formation of freshwater springs that well up from the aquifer. Twenty-five miles east of the C2C is **Crystal Springs**. Water from this spring is bottled under the brand name Zephyrhills, and you can find these plastic bottles of water in Florida grocery and convenience stores. The Zephyrhills company started bottling water from the springs in 1964. This enterprise remains controversial with regard to commercial water rights and the potential for depleting the aquifer. In 1987, the company, now owned by Nestlé, created a 530-acre preservation area surrounding the springs.

Pasco County's geology also makes it susceptible to **sinkholes**. In 2017, a massive sinkhole over 250 feet wide and 50 feet deep opened in a residential neighborhood in Land O' Lakes, six miles east of the C2C; eight homes became uninhabitable. This region is sometimes referred to as "sinkhole alley" due to the relative frequency of their formation. In Florida, sinkholes are often caused by erosion of underground lime rock. In many cases, the erosion process is slow, and a sinkhole depression forms gradually. Sometimes, gradual underground erosion creates an invisible cavity below the earth's surface. The roof of this unseen cavity can collapse abruptly and catastrophically, which is what scientists think happened in this 2017 event. Geologists continue to study sinkholes to better understand their cause and the impact of human activity on their formation and to identify locations where sinkholes can be expected.

This region of Florida provides habitat for several threatened and endangered species, including gopher tortoises (see preceding box), eastern indigo snakes, Florida Scrub Jays, and Red-cockaded Woodpeckers.

HISTORICAL NOTES

A visit to the **McNeill Homestead** in **Jay B. Starkey Wilderness Park** provides a glimpse into 1800s rural life. Not much remains of the house and farm that once was home to James McNeill and his family (sometimes spelled McNeil). Old, notched beams from the log cabin home as well as the remnants of animal pens and the family's freshwater well can be seen. A small family cemetery is also nearby. A glimpse into the hardships of the settler's rural life can be found in census and business records. In addition to working his small farm, McNeill took on jobs as a teacher and a carpenter. He outlived his two wives and a least one son who died in childhood. This land was purchased by Jay B. Starkey in 1936; by the 1970s and over the following decades, the Starkey family sold or donated acreage to ensure its preservation for future generations.

As the C2C winds along Starkey Boulevard, directly to the west is a community known as **Seven Springs**. An enterprising pioneer, Samuel H. Stevenson, created a small health resort here in 1913 by piping mineral water from one of the springs into a pool for those wishing to indulge in the purported benefits. Destroyed in a hurricane in 1921, the bathhouse was rebuilt, but by 1925, the land was sold for development. Today, while the Anclote River continues to run by the area, there is no evidence of the springs.

Like other regions in Florida, many early settlers of Pasco and Hernando Counties in the 1800s were farmers, citrus growers, and loggers. The major freezes in the late 1890s caused a significant decline in citrus production, and some citrus growers moved farther south. Timber and sawmills, however, were not subject to the whims of cold weather and continued to prosper throughout the 20th century. The C2C route in this area does not pass through the early settlement towns, many of which are farther inland by the rolling hills of Dade City, San Antonio, and Zephyrhills. To the west, along the Gulf of Mexico, the coastal towns of Hudson, Port Richey, and Aripeka were also settled in the late 1800s, taking advantage of the abundance of food resources provided by the Gulf as well as the opportunity to transport goods by sea.

TRAIL SECTION 7
TARPON SPRINGS TO CLEARWATER

NORTHERN PINELLAS COUNTY, INCLUDING THE TOWNS OF TARPON SPRINGS, DUNEDIN, AND CLEARWATER

Trail section length: 14 miles
Point A: 10 S. Safford Ave., Tarpon Springs
Point B: Cleveland Street District, 650 Cleveland St., Clearwater
4-mile optional spur trail to Honeymoon Island State Park
2.5-mile optional spur trail to Clearwater Beach

HIGHLIGHTS
Tarpon Springs town center
Tarpon Springs sponge docks
Dunedin town center
Wall Springs Park
Clearwater's Cleveland Street District

TRAILHEADS
Tarpon Springs town center (on-street parking)
(*continued below*)

Trail Section 7 — Tarpon Springs to Clearwater

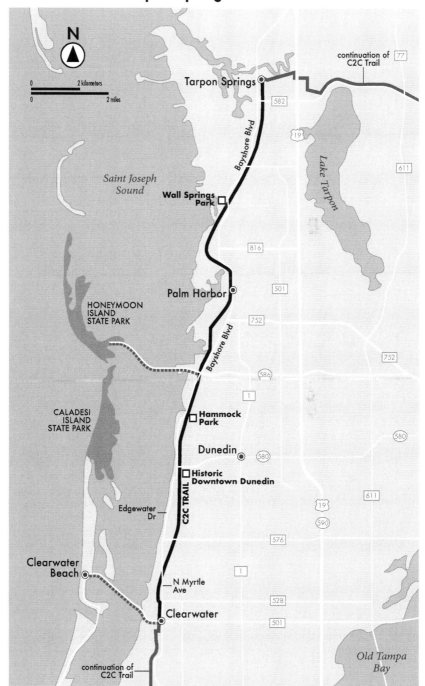

TRAILHEADS (continued)

Craig Park, 100 Beekman Ln., Tarpon Springs (0.5 mile west of the C2C)

Wall Springs Park, 3725 DeSoto Blvd., Palm Harbor

Dunedin Youth Guild Park, 2750 Bayshore Blvd., Dunedin

Hammock Park, 1900 San Mateo Drive, Dunedin

Josiah C. Weaver Park, 1258 Bayshore Blvd., Dunedin

Downtown Dunedin (on-street parking or in garage at 356 Monroe St.)

Coachman Park, 301 Drew St., Clearwater

Clearwater Cleveland Street District (on-street parking)

THE ROUTE: NEED TO KNOW

The C2C route follows the Fred Marquis Pinellas Trail for its entire length in Pinellas County. This trail is a favorite among locals because it is well marked, has numerous amenities, and is pleasant to ride. Trail Section 7 covers the northern part of the Pinellas Trail from Tarpon Springs to Clearwater.

The Pinellas Trail travels through one of the most densely populated counties of Florida, but 10 trail overpasses at busy intersections help to reduce interactions with motorized vehicles.

RECOMMENDED WALKS

In **downtown Tarpon Springs,** the C2C parallels Safford Avenue and runs down the street's median on the former railroad track. Combine a walk along the C2C here with an exploration of the town center of Tarpon Springs (note that this is not the area of the sponge docks). From the C2C, head west on Tarpon Avenue for 0.3 mile, and you'll reach the Spring Bayou. From here, walk in either direction on the shores of the bayou. Stately homes surround the bayou and reflect the prosperity of the town's beginnings. Return to the C2C on Orange Avenue, and you'll pass by the remarkable **Saint Nicholas Greek Orthodox Cathedral** (see "Local Culture" below). Many of the streets in this area have low traffic and sidewalks and are generally good for walking.

The Saint Nicholas Greek Orthodox Cathedral in Tarpon Springs, a local landmark, is ornately decorated with vibrant paintings and stained-glass windows. A statue in front commemorates the Epiphany divers.

For a lovely hike in natural "old" Florida adjacent to the C2C, head to **Hammock Park** (the official address is 1900 San Mateo Dr., but it is accessible from the C2C path via Buena Vista Drive North, Dunedin). A two-mile hike within the park takes you through the magnificent tree canopy. This 98-acre park boasts a lush forest with over 300 species of trees native to Florida. A total of five miles of boardwalks and hiking trails meander through the park, offering an immersive nature experience.

The C2C Trail through **Dunedin** is popular with walkers, runners, and skaters because of its attractive environment and the trail's proximity to restaurants, cafés, and shops. The one-mile trail section near the intersection of Main Street is usually the busiest. The half mile between **Main Street** and **Josiah Cephas Weaver Park** is particularly nice for a walk and has appealing destinations at each end.

Walking the 2.5-mile **spur trail to Clearwater Beach** offers spectacular views of Clearwater and the bay. By starting this walk at the intersection of the C2C and Cleveland Street in Clearwater, you will also get to explore a bit of Clearwater's town center, including the streetscaping and artwork along Cleveland Street. From the C2C at Cleveland Street, walk 0.5 mile west toward the harbor. When you reach the waterfront, turn left (south) and traverse Clearwater Memorial Park toward Pierce Street. A large spiral ramp for pedestrians and bicyclists takes you up onto the causeway. The entire length of the causeway is two miles, and at the western end, is bustling Clearwater Beach Pier 60. Where the path is close to the roadway, there is a concrete protection barrier between the path and motorized vehicles. This walk is popular with locals.

LOCAL CULTURE

There is no shortage of interesting things to see and do along the Pinellas County section of the C2C route. This trail is one of the original long-distance rail trails in Florida and provides cyclists and walkers many opportunities for sightseeing. Municipal officials, in conjunction with local artists, continue to find creative ways to enhance the trail experience. Most recently, the county demonstrated its ongoing commitment to the confluence of art, culture, and the trail through the **Pinellas Trail Mural Project**, which commissioned four artists to paint colorful murals on overpasses.

In **Tarpon Springs**, the trail runs down the median of Safford Avenue. Here, the C2C passes through a section of town that includes trailside cafés, small restaurants, and a bicycle shop. Just one block west, on the corner of Pinellas Avenue and Orange Street, lies the **Saint Nicholas Greek Orthodox Cathedral** (36 N. Pinellas Ave.). The Greek Orthodox parish was founded in 1907, and members assembled in a small church until this cathedral was completed in 1943. The building was designed using Istanbul's famous Hagia Sofia as a model. The ornate interior includes stained-glass windows and paintings of sacred images. Visitors are welcome, but hours are limited.

The **Historic Depot Museum** is adjacent to the C2C (160 E. Tarpon Ave.) at the corner of Safford Avenue and Tarpon Avenue.

Tarpon Springs–Downtown

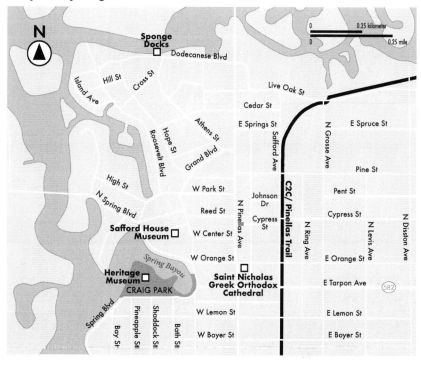

Once a train depot on the Orange Belt Railway, the building is now operated by the Tarpon Springs Area Historical Society. Portions of the interior have been restored to their original state as a working railway station, while other rooms contain local artifacts. The construction of this railroad, connecting Tarpon Springs to St. Petersburg in 1887, had a significant impact on the growth of Tarpon Springs.

For a short scenic detour, head west from Safford Street on Orange Street toward the **Spring Bayou**, and cycle or walk along the peaceful waterfront and the beautiful old homes. Around the east end of Spring Bayou, travel near the water's edge looking for birds or wildlife. In wintertime, this inlet is a welcoming place for manatees, which prefer the bayou's warm water on chilly days. For a real-time, online look at the bayou, and perhaps to see a manatee, access the city's "Spring Bayou Live Manatee Webcam" (https://www.ctsfl.us/cams/bayou/).

The Spring Bayou is also the location for the annual **Greek Orthodox Epiphany** celebration held on January 6. The local religious community holds a procession from St. Nicholas Cathedral down to the bayou. During the ceremony, a dove is released, and a cross is thrown into the water. Young men of the community, in a rite of passage, dive into the bayou in search of the cross; the one who retrieves it is said to be specially blessed for the upcoming year.

On the north side of the bayou sits the **Safford House Museum** (23 Parkin Ct.), a restored Victorian home built in 1883. The museum is filled with furniture and décor of its glory days and gives visitors a chance to experience the atmosphere of an elegant household of the era.

The **Heritage Museum** (100 Beekman Ln.) is in Craig Park at the south edge of the bayou. Displays include artifacts from indigenous tribes of the area, an exhibit about the local Greek community, and works by local artists.

The tourist highlight of Tarpon Springs is the Greek culture of **Dodecanese Boulevard** and the famous **Sponge Docks**, just a half mile away from the C2C route. In Tarpon Springs, Greek heritage and sponge-diving operations are inexorably linked: Greek immigrants were encouraged to move here over a hundred years ago for their sponge-diving expertise (see "Early Sponge Harvesting" box below). The town still has many Greek Americans living in it; the latest census reported that nearly 12 percent of its inhabitants identify as having Greek heritage. Along the touristy Dodecanese Boulevard, you'll find plenty of Greek restaurants and souvenir shops. Visitors can learn more about the town's sponge-diving culture by taking a boat tour, visiting the Tarpon Springs Aquarium, or stopping in at the Spongeorama, all of which can be found on Dodecanese Boulevard.

Early Sponge Harvesting

Sponges live throughout the world's oceans, but specific conditions such as those of Tarpon Springs are more favorable for their growth. The water here is clear and has high levels of nutrients, and the seabed has hard substrates that the sponges can latch on to.

When sponges were first harvested in this area in the mid-1800s, workers rowed out in small boats, carrying glass-bottom buckets and long poles with hooks at the end. Sponges were located by looking down into the water through the glass-bottom bucket, and the pole was then used to grab the sponges and haul them into the boat. Greek immigrants of the early 1900s brought with them extensive knowledge and experience in sponge harvesting. Their method was strikingly different: divers were sent down into the water and harvested the sponges by hand. Rubberized diving suits and metal helmets allowed divers to breathe through an air hose connected to the boat on the surface so they could stay submerged for long periods. The harvested sponges of Florida's west coast were then cleaned and shipped to markets throughout the country.

A sponge-harvesting boat at the famous Tarpon Springs Sponge Docks

Tarpon Springs hosts several festivals each year, including arts and crafts festivals and a renowned seafood festival as well as the January 6 Greek Orthodox Epiphany celebration.

Between Tarpon Springs and Dunedin, the C2C passes through **Palm Harbor**. Although you won't see much of the town from the trail, there are several restaurants and small shops just a block or two east of the path, especially in the half mile near the intersection of the C2C with Florida Avenue. Travel west 0.25 mile from the C2C on Florida Avenue, and you'll find **Pop Stansell Park** (797 Florida Ave.). On the shores of a bayou, it is a pleasant community park with a fishing pier, picnic facilities, and restrooms.

North of downtown Dunedin, make a stop at the **Andrews Memorial Chapel** in Hammock Park (1899 San Mateo Dr., Dunedin). From the trail, the short route to the chapel is just south of Cedar Creek, on Buena Vista Drive North. Head east on Buena Vista Drive for 300 feet. This 1888 chapel is on the National Register of Historic Places owing to its early-Florida architectural style and construction and its significance as one of the oldest surviving buildings in the area. Today, it is primarily a wedding and concert venue. Opening hours are limited, but you can walk around the chapel and its grounds and check out adjacent **Hammock Park** (see "Nature" below).

In the heart of **Dunedin**, particularly the C2C section between Skinner Boulevard to the north and Scotland Street to the south, are breweries, restaurants, ice cream shops, coffeehouses, and retail shops. Stop here to explore the quaint charm of this former train depot town, and partake in the edible delights. Dunedin was Florida's first officially designated "Trail Town," a recognition that honors the town's vibrant center and the amenities available to trail users. You can also find lodging nearby, either in a hotel or at a bed-and-breakfast. Check out the **Dunedin Downtown Market**, at the corner of Main Street and Douglas Avenue, for morning open-air markets that include fresh food and artisan crafts.

The **Dunedin History Museum** (349 Main St.), adjacent to the C2C, conserves Dunedin's past and keeps its heritage alive.

The museum is located in the town's original rail depot. Like other towns of this region, Dunedin's past is grounded in citrus and railroads. The town also played a vital role in World War II due to its production of citrus concentrate for soldiers and its role in training military tank operators. The "alligator tank," used as an amphibious lander in the war, was produced and field tested in Dunedin. This tank was initially designed by a civil engineer to operate in flooded or swampy areas to rescue people who were stranded by hurricanes. The military recognized the advantages of the tank and adopted it for their use.

To visit a waterfront marina with small shops and eateries nearby, head to Dunedin's **Edgewater Park** (51 Main St.). There, you'll find shaded benches, picnic facilities, and restrooms. Spend some time there to stroll by the waterfront and view the leisure boats at the docks.

The C2C route does not provide great views of the Gulf of Mexico, but that can be easily remedied by a short detour. Just three miles north of Dunedin, turn off the C2C, and bicycle out to **Honeymoon Island**. The causeway is busy with people walking, cycling, sunbathing, and fishing, and it is used as a base for water sports. For more details about this route, see "Optional Spur Trail to Honeymoon Island" below. If you're looking for unspoiled Gulf beaches, you'll find them here.

The trail navigates through an uninspired part of **Clearwater**, mostly municipal buildings, but it is worth going to the **Cleveland Street District**, bordering the trail. From the C2C, turn west on Cleveland Street, where you'll find the revitalized District, including restaurants, shopping, and entertainment venues. Continue west to the nearby harbor and marina if you want to get a look at the water. The distance from the intersection of C2C and Cleveland Street to the waterfront is about a half mile.

NATURE

Wall Springs Park (3725 DeSoto Blvd., Palm Harbor) is a lovely county park adjacent to the trail, approximately 3.5 miles south

127

of Tarpon Springs. Look for the entrance sign on the west side of the trail. This 200-plus-acre park offers shady paths among a natural setting and includes a boardwalk from which you can see a sheltered inlet, the Boggy Bayou. Along the shores of the bayou are excellent views of the mangroves. Head out past the spring and along the boardwalk that connects to a small island. At the northern end of this island is a lookout tower (less than a half mile from the spring). Climb the tower for a good view and a nice

Mangroves

Mangroves are shrubs or small trees that are particularly adapted to coastal environments. You can find them along Florida's coasts, as they grow in tidal conditions and can thrive in salty and brackish water along muddy shorelines.

Mangrove forests provide habitat for animals such as crabs, oysters, and barnacles. Birds and fish often feed among mangroves. In addition, they provide excellent protection of coastal lands against erosion from storm surges. Different varieties of mangroves are found in different environments, depending on salinity, water levels, and oxygen levels of the water.

In Florida, three types of mangrove species thrive: red (*Rhizophora mangle*), black (*Avicennia germinans*), and white (*Laguncularia racemosa*). All three species can be found in Wall Springs Park. Red mangroves have arching legs that bow out from the shrub. If their bark is scraped away, red wood is exposed. Black mangroves have skinny, fingerlike protrusions that grow upright out of the ground. Their bark is usually dark, sometimes blackish. White mangroves have rounded leaves, which distinguish them from the pointed leaves of red and black mangroves. White mangroves are so named because they often have white salty deposits on their leaves.

breeze. This park also has many picnic tables, a playground, small shelters, and restrooms.

This area has an interesting tale about the power of **hurricanes**. Florida's geography as a peninsula that juts into the warm waters of the Gulf of Mexico and the Atlantic Ocean's gulf stream makes it particularly vulnerable to hurricanes. In coastal areas, the peril is particularly high due to the possibility of a storm surge. In **1921 a massive hurricane** with winds over 140 mph made landfall near Tarpon Springs. The storm battered Pinellas County and the Tampa Bay area with extreme winds and severe flooding. Roads were washed out and massive amounts of property and crops were destroyed. The hurricane of 1921 left a long-lasting mark: it split Hog Island off the coast of Dunedin into two islands. Storm surge broke through the island, and the open-water pass created is known today as Hurricane Pass. The island to the south was subsequently named **Caladesi Island**, while the northern island became **Honeymoon Island**, which you can reach by bicycle (see "Optional Spur Trail to Honeymoon Island" below).

Hammock Park (1900 San Mateo Dr., but accessible from the C2C path via Buena Vista Drive North, Dunedin) provides an extraordinary opportunity to experience natural Florida. Hiking trails and a boardwalk take you among upland hardwood trees, ferns, sand pines, and palmettos to marshes and mangroves. Stop by the dedicated butterfly garden to see colorful plants and their pollinators. Fall and spring bird migrations bring in a wide variety of avian species, including warblers, buntings, and vireos, but the park reports that nearly 100 bird species call this park home year-round. Extensive studies have been conducted to identify the park's population of gopher tortoises, including the location of their burrows, and to plan for the preservation of their habitat. Hammock Park is also home to the charming Andrews Memorial Chapel (see "Local Culture" above).

Josiah Cephas Weaver Park (1258 Bayshore Blvd.) lies adjacent to the C2C just a half mile north of Dunedin and is a picturesque place to stop and relax. The park provides a shady respite with large trees, playground and exercise equipment, and picnic pavilions. For a view of the water, use the pedestrian crosswalk to cross Bayshore Boulevard to the waterfront and a 725-foot pier. From the pier, look for Ospreys and dolphins. The western view of St. Joseph Sound makes this a perfect spot to watch the sunset.

Traveling near the coast of the Gulf of Mexico provides an opportunity to see some of Florida's coastal birds. **Pelicans** are common in this area; their enormous bills and large bodies make them easy to identify. **Brown Pelicans** live here year-round. They can often be seen flying in a graceful V-formation overhead. These birds hunt fish by diving from the sky and plunging bill first into the water. **American White Pelicans** reside in Florida only during the winter months. Unlike brown pelicans, they feed on small fish by paddling on the water's surface, often driving fish into shallow water, then dipping their bills into the water to catch them. White pelicans will hunt cooperatively as a group, an interesting behavior to observe.

HISTORICAL NOTES

On the west coast of Florida along the Gulf of Mexico, numerous tidal inlets and rivers made this region hospitable to early humans. The abundance of food in the Tampa Bay estuary made it particularly suitable for supporting large numbers of people. Evidence of both the indigenous Weeden Island cultures and the later Tocobaga communities has been found in Pinellas County from as early as the first century CE. Shell mounds suggest that shellfish were a large part of their diet, and arrow tips indicate they probably also used bows and arrows for hunting.

In the 1500s, the west coast of Florida was scouted by Spanish explorer Pánfilo de Narváez and later by Hernando de Soto in their searches for gold and treasure. Neither expedition created settlements here but instead continued northward. For a compelling account of the ill-fated Narváez expedition, I recommend reading *A Land So Strange* by Andrés Reséndez. On this harrowing journey, only 4 of the more than 400 expedition members survived.

The story brings to life the expedition's hazards, including difficulties of navigation, storms, food supplies, and hostile interactions with the native residents.

Most permanent towns of Pinellas County (as well as other Florida regions) were not established until the 1800s after Spain ceded the peninsula to the United States. As a US territory, residents and officials lobbied for the construction of transportation projects. Improved infrastructure, combined with the forced removal of the Seminole Tribes (see "Historical Notes" in Section 5), opened territory for more settlers. The first public school of this area, an indication of the permanence of the new settlements, was erected in 1855 and built on the same location as present-day Clearwater High School.

Florida's State Stone: Agatized Coral

While traveling through Central Florida, you will notice an absence of rocks and boulders. Unlike other areas of North America, Florida has no igneous or metamorphic rocks. Florida's rocks are sedimentary, built up over time from compacted materials. Limestone, common in Florida, is an example of a sedimentary rock, but it is usually hidden from view by sand or vegetation.

When state officials designated a state stone in 1979, they chose agatized coral, which is not a true rock, but a fossil. Agatized coral fossil is created when silica found in water slowly seeps in and replaces the structure of ancient, buried coral. In essence, one mineral replaces another, keeping the shape of the first. Beautiful patterns and colors can be found when agatized coral geodes are split open and polished.

Agatized coral is found only in a few locations in the state, and one of the fortunate regions is the area surrounding Tampa Bay. The beaches of Honeymoon Island have long been known to fossil hunters as a place to search for agatized coral.

In the late 1800s, **Tarpon Springs** benefited from prosperous Northerners drawn to its alluring waterfront location and its accessibility due to the newly constructed railway. Affluent families built Victorian homes along the Spring Bayou, which quickly earned the name the "Golden Crescent," reflecting both the shape of the bayou and the prosperity of its new residents. Tarpon Springs flourished further with the influx of Greek immigrants who came here in the early 1900s as experts in sponge diving.

Dunedin also owes its success to its prime location on the coast of the Gulf of Mexico and the decision to put an Orange Belt Railway station here. Sailing ships made use of the substantial docks built by early settlers, creating a hub for commerce and transport. Originally called Jonesboro after an early settler, two Scottish immigrants petitioned to name the town Dunedin, derived from Dùn Èideann, the Scottish Gaelic name of Scotland's capital Edinburgh. The town's Scottish roots are kept alive today by the active **Scottish American Society** of Dunedin and through Scottish music concerts, highland dancers, a spring Highland Games Festival, and an autumn Celtic Festival.

The trail passes the historic Dunedin train depot in the center of town.

Clearwater is perhaps best known today for its access to beautiful Gulf beaches, but the city's name was inspired not by the beach but by crystal-clear freshwater springs. These springs once bubbled up from the aquifer in the area that is now Clearwater's business district. White settlers were drawn to the area in the 1840s, lured by the Federal Armed Occupation Act of 1842. Under this act, men over the age of 18 willing to work the land and defend it from indigenous people were given 160 acres. Cotton and vegetable farming was common, but the significant growth of Clearwater was thwarted by its remote location on this small peninsula until the railway was built in the 1880s.

Station Square Park (612 Cleveland St., Clearwater) is the location of the first train depot in Clearwater, built in 1888 for the Orange Belt Railway. The station was abandoned and demolished in the 1960s with the demise of the railway line. A historical marker for the depot can be found in this small park nestled among buildings in the downtown. Station Square Park is a pleasant place to stop and relax before visiting the nearby shops and restaurants.

By the time of the Florida real estate boom of the 1920s, Clearwater's town leaders were enthusiastic proponents of growth. Hotels welcomed tourists, and real estate developers touted the region's warm climate and proximity to beaches. By then, a bridge was built between the city and Clearwater Beach, allowing beachside development.

OPTIONAL SPUR TRAIL TO HONEYMOON ISLAND

Enjoy one of Florida's beautiful Gulf coast beaches by visiting this state park, accessible by a bike on a four-mile spur trail.

Four miles west of the C2C on the shore of the Gulf of Mexico is a superb state park beach. For the delight of seeing **Honeymoon Island State Park**, head to the intersection of the C2C and Curlew Road (SR 586) three miles north of the center of Dunedin. A shared-use spur trail heads west from this intersection to Honeymoon Island. Immediately after you turn west on SR 586, the road's name becomes Causeway Boulevard. The shared-use path is

Honeymoon Island Spur Trail

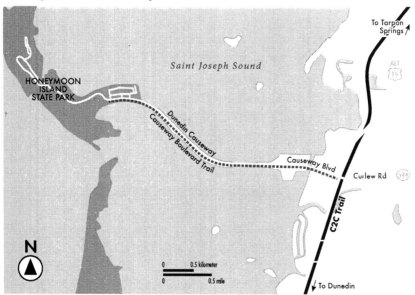

on the southern side of the causeway. This causeway is a local favorite and can be busy with walkers, runners, and cyclists, and for good reason: it heads out into the beautiful water of Saint Joseph Sound and to Honeymoon Island. Even before you get to Honeymoon Island, the causeway beaches are lively with sunbathers, swimmers, and boaters. Kayak rentals and casual eateries can be found here.

Keep traveling farther west, and you'll get to Honeymoon Island. Ride past the condominiums, and you'll soon reach the state park entrance (with a reduced fee for bicyclists and pedestrians). Once inside the park, take time to ride or walk along three miles of trails and enjoy the four miles of sandy beaches. Join the other swimmers and splash in the tempting water. Kayaks can be rented at the concession building, and the park's many pavilions invite you to stay for a picnic or rest break. Honeymoon Island is known for wildlife such as Ospreys, egrets, and herons. And if you're lucky, you may see less common birds such as Oystercatchers

Paths on Honeymoon Island lead you to beaches on the Gulf of Mexico.

and Roseate Spoonbills. Gopher tortoises also call this park home; look for them while traveling the inland paths.

A few sections of the otherwise sandy beaches of Honeymoon Island have rocklike cobbles. These limestone cobbles, some of which contain fossils, were dredged up from the nearby water in the 1960s and deposited on the southern end of the island. Dredging is still done in the area to maintain the island's beaches and keep Hurricane Pass navigable for boats.

If you have plenty of time and want to explore an unspoiled treasure of Florida, take a ferry to nearby **Caladesi Island State Park**, a beautiful park accessible only by boat. The ferry departs from Honeymoon Island. Visit the Caladesi Island Ferry website: https://caladesiferry.org.

OPTIONAL SPUR TRAIL TO CLEARWATER BEACH
From the city of Clearwater, it's possible to take the Memorial Causeway Bike Trail to Clearwater's beautiful beaches. From the C2C at Pierce Street, it is a 2.5-mile ride to Clearwater Beach's iconic Pier 60.

Clearwater Beach Spur Trail

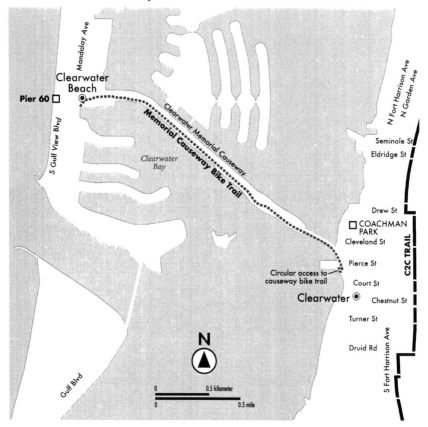

There are multiple ways to get to the Memorial Causeway Bike Trail, but perhaps the easiest from the C2C is to head west on Pierce Street (not a bike trail but lightly traveled by cars). As you near the water, the spiral path up to the bike trail is on your left; climb this spiral to arrive on the Memorial Causeway Bike Trail. The two-way bike trail is on the southwest side of the causeway. Stop along the causeway to savor the fantastic views of the intracoastal waterway, pleasure boats, and the town. The trail ends at the traffic circle at the intersection of Memorial Causeway

Boulevard and Coronado Drive. Immediately to the west and south is Clearwater Beach's famous Pier 60 with a large parking lot, playground, green space, and public restrooms. The 1,080-foot pier juts out into the Gulf of Mexico, and you'll find plenty of fishermen, walkers, and beachgoers. This is a great place to have a snack, enjoy a swim, or watch the sunset, all with an expansive view of the beautiful beach and the Gulf of Mexico.

While near the beach, consider going to the **Clearwater Marine Aquarium** (249 Windward Passage). The aquarium is accessible via a short bicycle path from the Memorial Causeway at the intersection of Island Way. At the aquarium, you'll learn about its conservation and research goals and meet rescued pelicans, sharks, sea turtles, and other marine life.

TRAIL SECTION 8
CLEARWATER TO ST. PETERSBURG

SOUTHERN PINELLAS COUNTY, INCLUDING THE TOWNS OF LARGO AND ST. PETERSBURG

Trail section length: 22 miles
Point A: Cleveland Street District, 650 Cleveland St., Clearwater
Point B: Pioneer Park, corner of First Avenue, S.E., and Bay
   Shore Drive, S.E., St. Petersburg

For information on Clearwater, see Trail Section 7.

HIGHLIGHTS
Florida Botanical Gardens and Heritage Village
St. Petersburg waterfront
St. Petersburg shopping and dining district
Arts and cultural centers and museums

TRAILHEADS
Clearwater's Cleveland Street District (on-street parking)
John S. Taylor Park, 1100 Eighth Ave., S.W., Largo
(*continued below*)

Trail Section 8 – Clearwater to St. Petersburg

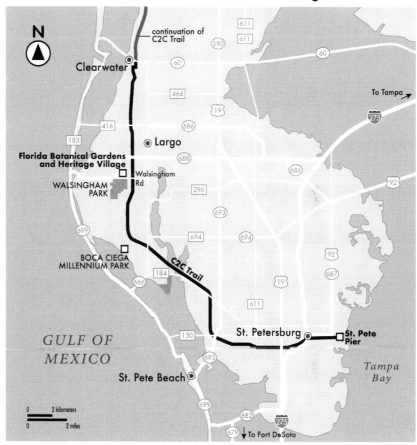

TRAILHEADS (continued)

Walsingham Park, Walsingham Rd., Largo (0.4 mile west of the C2C)

Blossom Lake Park, 10407 Blossom Lake Dr., Seminole

Seminole City Park, 7464 Ridge Rd., Seminole

Azalea Park, 1600 72nd St., N., St. Petersburg

Trailhead Park, 3800 Fairfield Ave., S., St. Petersburg

Downtown St. Petersburg (on-street parking and paid parking garages)

THE ROUTE: NEED TO KNOW

The C2C along the southern section of the Fred Marquis Pinellas Trail is well marked and easy to follow. Overpasses at busy intersections minimize encounters with motorized vehicles.

There is no official trailhead parking at either end of this segment, which begins and ends in city centers. In Clearwater, on-street parking is easy to find. In downtown St. Petersburg, look for on-street parking, or use one of the many parking garages.

RECOMMENDED WALKS

Much of the trail in this segment runs near neighborhoods and through commercial districts. Because of the population concentration of this area, there are fewer undeveloped areas along the C2C than in other segments. Some of the best walks combine the C2C with nearby park trails.

For a pleasant walk in Largo, start at the **John S. Taylor Park** trailhead (1100 Eighth Ave., S.W.) and walk around Taylor Lake, a 1.8-mile loop trail. Much of the loop is shaded, and this park has expanses of nature as well as picnic and play areas. Join the C2C at the northeast corner of the park on Eighth Avenue, and head north 0.75 mile to the quaint **Amish Country Store** (206 13th St., S.W.) for a takeout lunch or to pick up snacks.

For an extended Largo trek with facilities and points of interest at each end, walk between **John S. Taylor Park** (1100 Eighth Ave., S.W.) and the **Florida Botanical Gardens** (12211 Walsingham Rd.). This approximately three-mile (one-way) walk is primarily on the C2C; the half mile on Walsingham Road has wide sidewalks. Explore the botanical gardens and enjoy the plants and exhibits (see "Nature" below). For additional mileage, combine this walk with the hiking trails in **Walsingham Park**, just south of the Botanical Gardens. The Walsingham Park trails can add up to six miles of hiking.

Downtown St. Petersburg is very walkable and has a pleasing combination of parks, waterfront views, and historic buildings. For views of Tampa Bay, head north from the end of the C2C at

Downtown St. Petersburg by Bayshore Drive

Pioneer Park and walk along Bayshore Drive. The walk from Pioneer Park to Flora Wylie Park is 1.7 miles. You'll pass the famous and historic Vinoy Renaissance hotel, then enter a string of parks that offer green space, restrooms, some tree cover, sports fields, and expansive views of the bay.

A popular short walk is the half mile out to the end of the **St. Pete Pier**. The pier is a town focal point and is a great way to experience the local atmosphere with plenty to engage your senses. The St. Pete Pier begins at the intersection of Bayshore Drive and Second Avenue (see "Local Culture" below).

The C2C/Pinellas Trail runs parallel to First Avenue South in the downtown area. Combine a walk on the C2C with an excursion to **Mirror Lake,** just 0.25 mile north of the C2C at Sixth Street South. The 0.6-mile path around Mirror Lake is situated in a city park. This quiet oasis in the historic district is surrounded by many architecturally interesting buildings. The Mirror Lake Community Library at the northeast corner of Mirror Lake (280 Fifth St., N.) was built in 1915 in a style inspired by the French Beaux-Arts movement. It was funded by Andrew Carnegie as part of his nation-wide philanthropic library-building project, and it is still referred to by locals as **The Carnegie Library**. Head back to the C2C or walk one mile east on Second Avenue North to the St. Pete Pier. On the way to the pier, you will pass shops, restaurants, and Williams Park.

LOCAL CULTURE

In southern Pinellas County, the C2C passes through several municipalities, and it may not be obvious to trail riders when they leave one town and enter another. Rural buffer zones that once existed between towns have disappeared due to the population growth of this area. Pinellas County consistently ranks as the most densely populated county in Florida, with approximately 3,500 people per square mile. **Largo**, a geographically dispersed town, has undertaken a multiyear effort to revitalize its downtown core along **West Bay Drive**, which intersects the C2C. Among the infrastructure improvements are sidewalks and paths to encourage walking and bicycling. While there are plenty of restaurants, hotels, and shops throughout Largo, these revitalization efforts intend to create a focused, walkable downtown within a more compact district.

Largo also prides itself on its park system. Head east on West Bay Drive for 1 mile to reach **Largo Central Park** (101 Central Park Dr.). This 70-acre park in the center of town has playgrounds, walking paths, a performing arts center, picnic facilities, and restrooms. While here, visit the Historic Largo Feed Store & Museum (295 Central Park Dr.), one of the few historic buildings of the area, built in 1902.

Largo is home to the remarkable **Florida Botanical Gardens** and the adjacent **Heritage Village** (from the C2C, use the entrance at 12211 Walsingham Rd.). The botanical gardens celebrate both native flora and exotic plant species. At the Heritage Village, you'll find numerous historical buildings that preserve the stories of those who once lived and worked here. See "Nature" and "Historical Notes" below for more information.

Downtown St. Petersburg

N

Tampa Bay

St. Pete Pier

North Yacht Basin

Demens Landing Park

Bay Shore Dr

Beach Dr NE

Dali Museum

Dali Blvd

8th Ave SE

PIONEER PARK

Shopping and Dining District

7th Ave N

5th Ave N

3rd Ave N

2nd Ave N

1st Ave N

1st St SE

2nd St S

3rd St S

4th St S

Dali Blvd

Carnegie Library

Mirror Lake

C2C/PINELLAS TRAIL

2nd Ave S

3rd Ave S

4th Ave S

6th Ave S

8th St S

9th St S

7th Ave N

5th Ave N

Burlington Ave N

1st Ave N

Central Ave

1st Ave S

5th Ave S

7th Ave S

16th St S

C2C/PINELLAS TRAIL

0   0.25 kilometer

0   0.25 mile

Downtown **St. Petersburg** is a bustling city with a wide variety of restaurants, shops, museums, and lodging. The attractive and lively Beach Drive is a pedestrian-friendly street with plenty of places to eat, drink, shop, or simply sit and relax. The waterfront along Bayshore Boulevard and grassy parks are wonderful places to soak in the atmosphere of this small city. For nightlife, head to Beach Drive and Central Avenue. Outdoor events are commonly held in St. Petersburg's waterfront area, including farmers' markets, art strolls, outdoor movies, and music performances.

The **St. Pete Pier** is a vibrant focal point of the city. Completely rebuilt in 2020, this is not an ordinary fishing pier. In fact,

Monument on the St. Pete Pier honoring the first commercial passenger airline flight. The flight crossed Tampa Bay on its route from St. Petersburg to Tampa.

the pier and its associated park area cover 26 acres and offer something for everyone: pedestrian- and bicycle-friendly paths, splendid views of the bay, restaurants (both casual and upscale), open space for relaxing, boat docks, an enormous splash pad, and playgrounds. It's an excellent place to have a refreshing drink and to people watch. The **Tampa Bay Watch Discovery Center** is situated toward the end of the pier. Engage in its interactive exhibits and learn about Tampa Bay and the group's efforts to protect and restore its ecological health. The pier is a half mile long; if you've had enough walking or cycling for the day, hop on the free tram that runs up and down its length.

St. Petersburg is home to the famed **Salvador Dalí Museum** (1 Dalí Blvd.), which honors surrealist artist Salvador Dalí and his works. This museum boasts the world's second largest collection of Dalí's works, including oil paintings, drawings, sculptures, and watercolors (the largest collection is in his hometown of Figueres, Spain). The building itself is impressive with its immense sky-lit atrium and a sweeping spiral staircase. From the outside, huge glass domes seem to bubble up from solid concrete walls. Completed in 2011, the structure is designed to protect against hurricane and

The architecture of the Dalí Museum is as notable as the artwork inside.

flood damage; hence, the walls are made from concrete 18 inches thick. An outdoor garden contains interesting sculptures and plants and offers a place to enjoy the artistic scenery while catching breezes from the bay.

If you have more time to immerse yourself into the art world, visit the **Museum of Fine Arts** (255 Beach Dr., N.E.), which contains a vast collection including works by Monet, Rodin, and Wyeth. Exhibits include art and objects of ancient Greece and Rome, works by Native Americans, decorative glass art, European paintings, contemporary art, and more. For a museum with a narrower focus, stop at the **Chihuly Collection** (720 Central Ave.), which displays remarkable glass works of celebrated artist Dale Chihuly. The large-scale and colorful glassworks are sure to delight and inspire. This collection is part of the contemporary **Morean Arts Center** (719 Central Ave.).

If you are in town on a Saturday, the **St. Petersburg Saturday Morning Market** (100 First St., S.E.) is a dynamic scene that attracts a large assortment of merchants and shoppers. The market hosts over 100 vendors of fresh vegetables, baked goods, a wide

Fort DeSoto Park

Fort DeSoto Park is renowned for its world-class beaches, windsurfing, kitesurfing, bird-watching opportunities, and fitness trails. Many running races and triathlons are held here. Fort DeSoto Park is not on the C2C Trail but can be reached by bicycle by taking the Skyway Trail south and heading west on the connecting Bayway Trail. At its closest, it is approximately 13 miles from the C2C to the park entrance, and within the park, are several more miles of bicycle and pedestrian trails. Visitors can rent canoes and kayaks, and campsites are available. Enjoy the pleasure of the waterfront beaches and marshes or explore the historic fort, constructed in 1898.

variety of food from an array of cultures, artisanal crafts, and live music.

NATURE

Much of the trail along this section runs through neighborhoods and business districts. But several locations along the route provide excellent opportunities to enjoy and experience nature.

Walsingham Park is the largest park along this segment of the route. From the C2C at the intersection of Walsingham Road, travel west on Walsingham Road for 0.5 mile. Walsingham Road has both bicycle lanes and wide sidewalks along this half-mile stretch. Inside the park, a bicycle loop travels around the Walsingham Reservoir. There are a total of six miles of shared-use paths and quiet roads within the park. Picnic shelters and restrooms are also available. Look for wildlife in the park such as birds, alligators, and gopher tortoises. Note that while the park's official entrance address is 12615 102nd Avenue, Seminole, the easiest and shortest entrance from the C2C is on Walsingham Road.

The beautiful **Florida Botanical Gardens** are just a half mile west of the C2C in Largo. Use the entrance at 12211 Walsingham Road across from Walsingham Park entrance. From this entrance, follow the nature path northward, and then cross over McKay Creek to the west gardens. As you wander through the 100-plus acres, take your time to explore the variety of themed gardens abounding in tropical plants, butterfly and pollinator attractors, herbs, cacti, palms, and Florida native plants. This property is also home to the Heritage Village (see "Historical Notes" below).

A one-mile bicycle/pedestrian bridge on the C2C crosses **Long Bayou** (the bridge is approximately 12 miles south of Clearwater and 10 miles from the trail terminus in St. Petersburg). Long Bayou carries water out to **Boca Ciega Bay** and the Gulf of Mexico. The bayou's watershed covers over 40 square miles, including many lakes, ponds, rivers, and canals. This shallow inland waterway is an excellent place for fishing, kayaking, and canoeing. Its proximity to a densely populated area makes it vulnerable to pollution,

Anoles

Small lizards abound in Florida and are often seen scurrying on patios, on top of railings, or on plants. The species seen most often is the brown anole (*Anolis sagrei*), which was introduced to the state from Cuba or the Bahamas. The Florida native green anole (*Anolis carolinensis*) is less common but can easily be identified by its distinctive bright green color. These two species eat the same types of food and share many behaviors. Scientists have observed that when territorial conflicts arise between the two, the green anoles often relocate high in trees, while the brown anoles retain the ground territory. Usually, the anoles you'll see will be four to five inches long. Anoles have detachable tails; if caught by a predator, they can release the tail, enabling them to escape. The tail will usually grow back over time.

and Pinellas County works with other municipalities and agencies to protect this valuable watershed and habitat.

Noteworthy **Boca Ciega Millennium Park** (12410 74th Ave., N., Seminole) is an easy half mile west of the C2C. This appealing park makes a perfect break approximately halfway between Clearwater and St. Petersburg. Turn west from the trail at the intersection of 74th Avenue (look for a Seminole city park and playground that are located at this intersection). This avenue has low to moderate traffic, but if you prefer, you can use the sidewalk for the half-mile ride to the park entrance. Inside the park, a bicycle path leads to quiet park roads by the shore of **Boca Ciega Bay**.

Boca Ciega Millennium Park exclusively uses Florida native plants in its landscaping. And in heavily populated Pinellas County, this is one of the few places to get a close look at an unspoiled coastal environment. You'll find ecosystems such as mangrove swamps, salt marshes, coastal oak hammocks, and pine flatwoods. A boardwalk travels along the shore of Boca Ciega Bay, and the 35-foot observation tower provides wide open views. You will also find picnic pavilions, restrooms, playground facilities, and a kayak/canoe launch. Ancient fossils were discovered at this location, shedding light on the prehistoric environment of the area (see "Historical Notes" below).

HISTORICAL NOTES

An amazing collection of **fossils** was discovered in 2007 at **Boca Ciega Millennium Park**. A local high school student was photographing rocks when she found an unusual object and took it to experts. It was a mammoth's tooth. Paleontologists from Florida colleges and universities as well as community volunteers were called in to excavate the site and identify the large number of unearthed fossils. These fossils date back 12,000 to 18,000 years to the late Pleistocene, the era of the last ice age period, and include Colombian Mammoths, giant bison, llamas, tortoises, and giant armadillos. Because of the types of fossils that were identified, scientists believe that this was an area of open grassland or prairie, which is unusual compared to other Florida fossil sites. The Boca Ciega collection is currently housed at the state's Museum of Natural History in Gainesville. Unfortunately, dinosaur enthusiasts won't find any dinosaur fossils in Florida. The state's oldest surface rocks date back to between 30 and 35 million years ago; dinosaurs became extinct long before that, approximately 65 million years ago.

From the time of the last ice age (12,000 years ago), early humans probably lived in this coastal region near modern-day Tampa Bay. Little evidence of their presence endured, except spear points from that era. However, after humans developed the ability to create ceramic items, typically pots, they unknowingly left behind traces for future generations to study. The distinct characteristics of ceramics, made for both ceremonial and functional use, can be used to identify the culture and time frame of its creators. Archaeologists believe that the pottery excavated from the

Weedon Island Preserve, in eastern Pinellas County, belonged to the Manasota indigenous culture from the first century CE.

By the time Spanish and French explorers came to Florida in the 1500s, the Weeden Island, Manasota, and related Safety Harbor cultures had been displaced by the **Tocobaga** people. Evidence of the Tocobaga Tribe can be found in the large mounds they built. While some mounds were simply made of discarded shells and trash, others were burial or ceremonial grounds. Some of the mounds are still visible, including the Pinellas Point Temple Mound, Weedon Island Mounds, and the Safety Harbor Temple Mound, all of which are situated on the shores of Tampa Bay but not directly on the C2C route. By the late 17th century, the people of the Tocobaga culture had disappeared, likely due to a combination of factors including the diseases brought by European explorers, warfare, or assimilation into other cultures.

The settlement of Pinellas County in the 1800s by Europeans was due in large part to the same reason indigenous people were drawn here: the abundance of natural resources. After Florida became a territory and then a state, entrepreneurs and pioneers demanded better transportation systems, and the roads and railways that met that demand paved the way for even more settlers. **Peter Demens**, the Russian-born businessman, was one of these ambitious newcomers. Demens moved to this region in search of inexpensive land and money-making opportunities and was the driving force behind the Orange Belt Railway (see earlier discussion "Florida's Heritage Along the C2C Path"). Demens's desire to name a town in Florida after his Russian homeland came to fruition when the town of St. Petersburg, Florida, officially chose its name in 1888.

To explore the history of Pinellas County, visit the **Heritage Village** (from the C2C, use the entrance at 12211 Walsingham Rd., Largo) located on the same property as the Florida Botanical Gardens. This collection of historical area buildings is part of Pinellas County's efforts to preserve and share the stories of its history. The village includes an 1852 log cabin, sugarcane mill,

This antique truck is one of the many artifacts at the Pinellas County Heritage Village.

smokehouse, boat shop, sponge warehouse, general store from 1915, replica schoolhouse, and Sulphur Springs train depot. This is a pleasant place to wander, absorb the atmosphere, and learn about the bygone days of Pinellas County and how earlier residents lived.

In 1914, the world's **first commercial passenger airplane flight** took off from St. Petersburg. The 22-minute seaplane flight between St. Petersburg and Tampa was a substantial time savings for a trip that normally took many hours by boat or railway. Head to **Benoist Plaza** on the **St. Pete Pier** to see the full-size airplane sculpture and read the story of the flight. The plane was called a "boat plane" or "airboat" because it took off and landed on water. Although the scheduled flights lasted only a few months, they helped pave the way for future passenger air travel.

After World War I and before the Great Depression, Pinellas County experienced a real estate boom, during which land prices exploded and several stunning resort hotels were built. Several of these **iconic hotels** in St. Petersburg can be seen today, including the **Vinoy** (501 Fifth Ave., N.E.) and the Princess Martha (411 First Ave., N., currently an apartment building). The famous **Don CeSar** (3400 Gulf Blvd., St. Pete Beach), which bills itself as a "monument to glamour and leisure," was also built at this time. The Gandy Bridge was completed in 1924, connecting St. Petersburg to Tampa, dramatically reducing the travel time between these two cities and fueling the growth of Pinellas County.

Just two blocks north of the C2C, in downtown St. Petersburg, is the unique and beautiful **Open Air Post Office** (400 First Ave., N.). Built in 1917, the building was designed and championed by the local postmaster, who wanted residents to have 24-hour access to their post office boxes and saw no need to enclose it given the region's climate. The Mediterranean Revival–style architecture features a series of arches with intricate ornamental design. Because of its unique open-air design and interesting architecture, the building is listed on the National Register of Historic Places.

The **Orange Belt Railway** ushered in an era of growth and economic opportunity for Pinellas County and St. Petersburg in the late 1800s; over a hundred years later, the long-abandoned tracks needed a new purpose. Citizens of Pinellas County recognized the value of the abandoned railroad property, and through a concerted multiyear effort by many individuals and municipalities, the Pinellas Trail was born in 1990. As one of the first long-distance rail trails in Florida, its popularity energized a movement to create more trails and to ultimately connect them to create this unique and inviting coast-to-coast trail across Florida.

PRACTICAL PLANNING: SUGGESTED ITINERARIES AND RESOURCES

HOTEL LODGING

Hotels can be found near the C2C in the locations listed below. Check the internet for additional listings. Also consider alternative lodging resources such as Airbnb or through Booking.com, which lets you search by a variety of options.

DeBary: near the intersection of the C2C and I-4 (Hampton Inn, Travelodge)

Sanford: outside of town near the intersection of I-4 and Highway 46 (Springhill Suites, Comfort Inn, Holiday Inn, WoodSpring Suites)

Sanford: Thurston House B&B and boutique lodging in the historic downtown

Lake Mary: intersection of International Parkway and H.E. Thomas, Jr. Parkway (Weston, Hampton Inn, Marriott)

Lake Mary: intersection of International Parkway and Lake Mary Boulevard (Courtyard by Marriott, Hyatt Place)

Winter Garden: boutique hotel in downtown historic district (Edgewater Hotel)

Minneola: along Lake Minneola near Clermont (Lake Minneola Inn)

Clermont: outside of town, south of the C2C along SR 50 (Holiday Inn, Fairfield Inn)

Brooksville: outside of town, near the intersection of SR 50 and I-75 (Hampton Inn, Quality Inn, Holiday Inn, Microtel)

Spring Hill: near the intersection of SR 50 and the Suncoast Parkway SR 589 (sometimes called Brooksville or Brookridge area) (Holiday Inn, Fairfield Inn)

Trinity/Odessa: along SR 54, east of the C2C (Hampton Inn, Holiday Inn Express)

Tarpon Springs: along US 19 (Hampton Inn, Tarpon Shores Inn)

Tarpon Springs: within a half mile of the C2C (1910 Inn, Ashley's Victorian Haven B&B)

Dunedin: near causeway to Honeymoon Island (Hampton Inn, Palm Court Motel)

Dunedin: near intersection of Main Street and Broadway (Holiday Inn, Best Western, Beyond the Wall B&B, Meranova B&B)

Clearwater: downtown near Court Street (Residence Inn, Tropical Inn)

Clearwater Beach: many hotels (15 plus) on Coronado Drive

St. Petersburg: many hotels in downtown area (12 plus, including most major chains)

At the time of publication, there are **two lengthy sections without standard hotels**: the 38-mile stretch between Titusville and DeBary and the 36-mile stretch between Clermont and Brooksville.

CAMPGROUNDS

The following campgrounds are along or very close to the C2C:

Titusville/Kennedy Space Center KOA Journey (Trail Section 1)

Hickory Bluff Preserve, organized groups only; permit required (Trail Section 2)

Gemini Springs Park (Trail Section 2)

Lake Monroe Park (Trail Section 2)

Clarcona Horse Park (Trail Section 4)

Hog Island Recreation Area, Withlacoochee River, Bushnell (Trail Section 5)

Silver Lake/Crooked River Campground, Croom Area, 31475 Silver Lake Rd., Brooksville (Trail Section 5)

Cypress Glen Campground, 31475 Silver Lake Rd., Brooksville (Trail Section 5)

J. B. Starkey Wilderness Park (Trail Section 6)

Clearwater/Lake Tarpon KOA (Trail Section 7)

St. Petersburg/Madeira Beach KOA (Trail Section 8)

SUGGESTED ITINERARY FOR A TWO-DAY NOVICE CYCLE TOUR

For novice cycle tourists or those traveling with youngsters, try an out-and-back two-day tour on the C2C with one overnight stay. Good options for a short and fun beginner's trip, with hotel lodging and an interesting destination, include:

Dunedin–Tarpon Springs (11 miles each way)

Winter Garden–Clermont (13 miles each way)

St. Petersburg–Dunedin (25 miles each way)

SUGGESTED ITINERARIES BASED ON HOTEL LODGING

Itinerary A: 6 days riding, 5 overnights

Titusville to DeBary, 38 miles

DeBary to Clermont, 53 miles

Clermont to Brooksville (at SR 50 & I-75), 36–50 miles (varies based on "gap" route)

Brooksville (at SR 50 & I-75) to Spring Hill at Suncoast Parkway, 25 miles

Spring Hill at Suncoast Parkway to Tarpon Springs, 46 miles

Tarpon Springs to St. Petersburg, 35 miles

Itinerary B: 5 days riding, 4 overnights:
Titusville to DeBary, 38 miles
DeBary to Clermont, 53 miles
Clermont to Spring Hill at Suncoast Parkway, 57–65 miles (varies based on "gap" route)
Spring Hill at Suncoast Parkway to Dunedin, 58 miles
Dunedin to St. Petersburg, 26 miles

Itinerary C: 5 days riding, 4 overnights:
Titusville to Sanford, 47 miles
Sanford to Winter Garden, 36 miles
Winter Garden to Brooksville (at SR 50 & 1-75), 48–58 miles (varies based on "gap" route)
Brooksville (at SR 50 & I-75) to Tarpon Springs, 67 miles
Tarpon Springs to St. Petersburg, 35 miles

Itinerary D: 4 days riding, 3 overnights
Titusville to Lake Mary, 53 miles
Lake Mary to Clermont, 39 miles
Clermont to Springhill at Suncoast Parkway 56–65 miles (varies based on "gap" route)
Springhill at Suncoast Parkway to St. Petersburg, 84 miles

Itinerary E: 3 days riding, 2 overnights
Titusville to Clermont, 92 miles
Clermont to Springhill at Suncoast Parkway 56–65 miles (varies based on "gap" route)
Springhill at Suncoast Parkway to St. Petersburg, 84 miles

BE SURE TO EXPLORE: PLACES TO VISIT BASED ON INTEREST

Each section of the C2C has something for everyone: beautiful natural areas, local art, historic buildings, or a unique setting for eating and dining. But for those with specific interests, the following provides a quick reference for places where you'll want to spend extra time along the way.

Itinerary Focus: Local Atmosphere and Culture
Sanford town center (Trail Section 3, via spur trail)

Winter Garden town center (Trail Section 4)
Tarpon Springs town center and sponge docks (Trail Section 7)
Dunedin town center (Trail Section 7)
St. Petersburg city center (Trail Section 8)

Itinerary Focus: Nature
Merritt Island National Wildlife Refuge (Trail Section 1)
Gemini Springs Park (Trail Section 2)
Oakland Nature Preserve (Trail Section 4)
Withlacoochee State Forest (Trail Section 5)
Brooker Creek Preserve (Trail Section 6)
J. B. Starkey Wilderness Preserve (Trail Section 6)
Wall Springs Park (Trail Section 7)
Honeymoon Island State Park (Trail Section 7)

Itinerary Focus: Local History
Titusville: Aerospace & Early Settlers (Trail Section 1)
Sanford: Steamboats & Agriculture (Trail Section 3)
Winter Garden: Citrus & Railways (Trail Section 4)
Brooksville: Plantations & Railways (Trail Section 5)
Tarpon Springs: Greek Settlers & Sponge Diving
    (Trail Section 7)
Dunedin: Scottish Settlers & Railways (Trail Section 7)
St. Petersburg Area: Indigenous Cultures & Spanish Explorers
    (Trail Section 8)

TAKE ADVANTAGE OF SUNRAIL

Central Florida's light rail system, SunRail, is easy to use, and bicycles are permitted on the train with no extra fee. The system is a commuter rail system, which means that the hours, days, and frequency of operation cater to commuters, with more trains running in the morning and late afternoon/early evening and only on weekdays. For train schedules, check https://sunrail.com.

SunRail is ideal for Central Florida bicyclists or walkers who want to enjoy the C2C and perhaps explore new territory. Take the train to the DeBary station, and from there, you can ride your bicycle on the C2C east toward Titusville or head west to Clermont. For hikers and walkers, the DeBary station offers easy access to Gemini Springs Park (see Trail Section 2). As out-and-back one-day excursions, the rides or walks can be as long or short as you want.

For visitors traveling on the C2C, SunRail can be used from the DeBary station to reach destinations not on the C2C such as Lake Mary, Maitland, Winter Park, Orlando, Kissimmee, and Poinciana. You could take an excursion to downtown Orlando, spend the night, then head back to DeBary on SunRail the next day and continue the C2C journey.

THE AUTHOR'S FAVORITES

Here are a few of my favorite places to stop along the C2C path. As you plan your travels, think of spending extra time at some of these:

White Sands Buddhist Center in Mims, for its peaceful gardens and magnificent statuary (Trail Section 1)

Gemini Springs Park, for its lush landscape and geological features (Trail Section 2)

Winter Garden's town center, for its lively, walkable, bicycle-friendly atmosphere with plenty of places to eat (Trail Section 4)

Oakland Nature Preserve, for its window into beautiful, natural Florida and the boardwalk to Lake Apopka (Trail Section 4)

Clermont Waterfront Park, for its vibrant activity, views of Lake Minnehaha, and the Historic Village (Trail Section 4/5)

Brooker Creek Preserve, for its expansive wilderness and informative Education Center (Trail Section 6)

Dunedin Town Center, for its trail-centered restaurants, breweries, shops, and quaint atmosphere (Trail Section 7)

St. Petersburg, for its vibrant downtown area, family-friendly parks and pier, good restaurants, and lively arts scene (Trail Section 8)

ENCOUNTERS WITH FLORIDA'S ANIMALS

The most dangerous animals you are most likely to encounter while riding the C2C are squirrels: they'll dart across the path unpredictably. Be prepared for mosquitos, too, especially at dawn and dusk. As for alligators, they prefer the water but will sun themselves along the shores of lakes and rivers, especially on chilly, sunny days. You are very unlikely to find any on the paved C2C path. Florida black bears are uncommon and tend to shy away from people, so it is also improbable you'll see one. Enjoy encounters with all wild animals, including birds and tortoises, from a respectful distance, and remember never to feed wild animals.

SUGGESTED READING

If you would like to enhance your C2C journey, I recommend the following books that are set in Florida and capture its essence.

A Land Remembered by Patrick D. Smith. A best-selling novel about the Florida frontier spanning three generations from the mid-1800s through the mid-1900s. This work features early Florida settlers and cattlemen living among formidable swamps, mosquitos, and hurricanes.

Devil in the Grove: Thurgood Marshall, the Groveland Boys, and the Dawn of a New America by Gilbert King. This Pulitzer Prize–winning book is a nonfiction account of the events surrounding the false accusation and trial of four young Black men charged with raping a white woman in Central Florida in 1949.

Their Eyes Were Watching God by Zora Neal Hurston. Hurston (1891–1960) grew up in Eatonville, Florida, just a few miles southeast of the C2C path. This novel, published in 1937, is perhaps her most notable work. It tells the story of Janie, an African American woman, and explores issues such as gender roles, love, and domestic violence. The story is set both in Eatonville and the Florida Everglades.

More notable books with distinctive Florida settings:

Cross Creek by Marjorie Kinnan Rawlings
Florida by Lauren Goff
A Land So Strange: The Epic Journey of Cabeza de Vaca by Andrés Reséndez
Oranges by John McPhee
The Orchid Thief by Susan Orleans
Sanibel Flats by Randy Wayne White
Swamplandia by Karen Russell
Tourist Season by Carl Hiaasen

ADDITIONAL RESOURCES
Online Maps
100 Florida Trails. Maps, photos, and trail descriptions: https://www.100floridatrails.com.

Facebook C2C dedicated group pages, especially "Florida Coast to Coast (C2C) Trail." This page has links to maps as well as helpful discussions.

Florida Department of Transportation and Tampa Bay Regional Planning Council, updates on trail segments: http://c2cconnector.org.

Florida Department of Transportation. C2C status map of incomplete sections: https://floridadep.gov/sites/default/files/suntrail_c2c_connectinggaps_2021-10_0.pdf.

Florida Office of Greenways and Trails, Coast-to-Coast Trail map: https://floridadep.gov/parks/ogt/content/florida-coast-coast-trail.

Florida Hikes. Hiking, bicycling, camping maps and information. https://floridahikes.com.

Florida Department of Environmental Protection. Bicycling, hiking, and paddling trail maps: https://floridadep.gov/parks/ogt/content/online-trail-guide.

Google Maps. Use the "biking" layers option. https://www.google.com/maps.

Map My Ride. Routes and routing planning software: https://www.mapmyride.com.

Ride with GPS. Plan, find, and record routes. https://ridewithgps.com.

TopographicMap.com. Visualize the elevation changes of the state: https://en-gb.topographic-map.com/maps/f5e4/Florida.

Other Internet Resources

Airbnb. An alternative to hotels or campgrounds. Lodging provided by private hosts: https://www.airbnb.com.

The Florida Bicycle Association. Supports and promotes bicycling in Florida: https://floridabicycle.org.

Warmshowers. Network of hosts and lodging for touring bicyclists: https://www.warmshowers.org.

APPENDIX: CROSSING THE GAP BETWEEN GROVELAND AND BROOKSVILLE

At the time of publication, there is a substantial gap in the C2C route between Groveland and the Withlacoochee Trail. The 28-mile projected trail in this section will generally align with SR 50.

The east end of the gap is in Groveland near the intersection of SR 565A and Silver Eagle Road, approximately 0.7 mile north of SR 50.

The west end of the gap is at the intersection of the Withlacoochee Trail and SR 50 (look for the intersection of Croom Rital Road and SR 50).

Inexperienced riders or those who prefer not to ride on roads should find an alternative method of crossing the gap, such as renting a vehicle or having a friend provide a shuttle, or segment ride completed sections only.

Construction is already underway on some segments of this gap, especially in Hernando County. The final completion of this gap is scheduled for 2026. For updates on the construction status, go to https://floridadep.gov/sites/default/files/suntrail_c2c _connectinggaps_2021-10_0.pdf.

Until the gap is completed, some cyclists have found alterna-tive, unofficial routes to ride across the gap. To review some of these routes, search on programs such as Ride with GPS, Strava, or Map My Ride. None of these routes are official or sanctioned. Riding on roads with vehicular traffic is very different from riding on trails and requires different skills. In some cases, the alternative route passes through remote areas on dirt roads.

Provided below are some route options found by other cyclists, all of which include riding on roads without designated bicycle lanes. These do not have any route signage. Many iterations of these alternate routes can be found online through route mapping programs. These routes are not suitable for inexperienced riders. Cyclists who decide to ride across the gap do so at their own risk.

GAP CROSSING: STRADDLE SR 50 ROUTE

For a detailed map of this fully paved gap option, go to Map My Ride and search for "FL C2C Gap-Straddle SR 50 Route." This route is 44 miles and, of the options, is perhaps the best in terms of automotive traffic and good road surfaces. Between Groveland and Linden, the route is mostly south of SR 50. From Linden on to Webster, Nobleton, and the Withlacoochee Trail, the route is north of SR 50. For about 1.5 miles east of Mabel, the route uses the shoulder of SR 50. Link: https://www.mapmyride.com/routes/view/4767131593.

GAP CROSSING: GREEN SWAMP ROUTE

For a detailed map of a gap option that is 50 percent unpaved, go to Map My Ride, and search for "FL C2C Gap - Green Swamp Route." This route is 38 miles. For those who want to avoid automotive traffic as much as possible, this route fits the bill. Note that in the easternmost portion of the Green Swamp's Richloam Wildlife Management Area, near the Van Fleet Trail's Bay Lake Trailhead, there is about 1.5 miles of sand or soft dirt; you will probably have to push your bike through this. But the other roads in the Richloam WMA on this route are hard-packed dirt (Lacoochee Clay Sink Rd., S. Grade Rd., and Center Grade Rd.). The 17 miles across the Richloam WMA are very remote with no facilities. Limited hunting is permitted; check the hunting schedule. The route joins the Withlacoochee Trail in Trilby, which connects to the Good Neighbor Trail. Link: https://www.mapmyride.com/routes/view/4767155440.

GAP CROSSING: NORTHERN ROUTE

For a detailed map of another fully paved gap option, go to Map My Ride, and search for "C2C Gap Center Hill Northern Route." This 38-mile route takes a more northern path passing through the towns of Center Hill, Bushell, and Nobleton. Note that highways CR469 and SR48 have fast-moving traffic and very narrow shoulders. CR469 can be avoided by taking a longer route using SR33, Austin Merritt Road, and Youth Camp Road. Link: https://www.mapmyride.com/routes/view/4767162319.

GAP CROSSING: SR 50 ROUTE

The eventual completed trail across the gap will generally align with SR 50. Riders have crossed the gap by staying on SR 50. Because of the high volume of motorized traffic, many share the opinion that it is not a suitable cycling route until the off-road shared-use path is built. Only some sections of SR 50 have shoulders. This route is 28 miles.

SOURCES AND REFERENCES

Asukile, Imani D. *Hernando County, Florida, Black America Series.* Charleston: Arcadia Publishing, 2005.

Bates, Michael D. *Etna Camp Casts Spotlight on Other Local Landmarks.* Chronicle Online, July 19, 2019.

Brotemarkle, Benjamin D. *Beyond the Theme Parks: Exploring Central Florida.* Gainesville: University Press of Florida, 1999.

Brown, Robin C. *Florida's First People.* Sarasota: Pineapple Press, 1994.

Bryan, Jonathan R., Thomas M. Scott, and Guy H. Means. *Roadside Geology of Florida.* Missoula: Mountain Press, 2008.

Clark, James C. *A Concise History of Florida.* Charleston: The History Press, 2014.

Cannon, Jeff, "Who Was James McNeill?" *The Patch,* July 24, 2011. https://patch.com/florida/newportrichey/who-was -james-mcneill.

Davis, Jack E. "Florida by Nature: A Survey of Extrahuman Historical Agency," in *The History of Florida,* ed. Michael Gannon. Gainesville: University of Florida Press, 2018.

Florida Fish and Wildlife Conservation Commission, https:// myfwc.com.

Florida Nature Coast, http://floridanaturecoast.org.

Gannon, Michael, ed. *The History of Florida.* Gainesville: University of Florida Press, 2018.

Hensley, Donald. "History of the Orange Line." *Trains*, April 1, 2011. https://www.trains.com/trn/train-basics/ask-trains/history-of-the-orange-line.

Johnson, Miriam W., and Rosemary Y. Young. *Clermont: Gem of the Hills.* Tallahassee: Rose Publishing Co., 1984.

Kambic, Randy. "Soak Up History Like a Sponge in Tarpon Springs." *The News-Press*, November 16, 2014. https://www.news-press.com/story/life/outdoors/2014/11/15/soak-history-like-sponge-tarpon-springs/19087565.

King, Gilbert. *Devil in the Grove: Thurgood Marshall, the Groveland Boys, and the Dawn of a New America.* New York: Harper Perennial, 2012.

Martinez, Robert. *Images of America: Brooksville.* Charleston: Arcadia Publishing, 2004.

Nelson, Gill. *The Trees of Florida.* Sarasota: Pineapple Press, 2017.

Pratts, J. J. *The Historical Marker Database.* https://www.hmdb.org.

Reséndez, Andrés. *A Land So Strange: The Epic Journey of Cabeze de Vaca.* New York: Basic Books, 2009.

Robison, Jim, and Mark Andrews. *Flashbacks: The Story of Central Florida's Past.* The Orange County Historical Society and the Orlando Sentinel, 1995.

Sibley, David Allen. *The Sibley Field Guide to Birds of Eastern North America.* New York: Knopf, 2012.

Tebeau, Charlton W. *A History of Florida.* Miami: University of Miami Press, 1971.

Wise, Madonna Jervis. *A Haunted History of Pasco County.* Charleston, SC: The History Press, 2020.

INDEX

Page numbers for photographs are in bold.

"Trail Towns," 4

100 Florida Trails, 10, 160
1885 Train Depot, 94

A Land Remembered, 48, 159
A. Max Brewer Bridge, 20
A. Max Brewer Causeway
    Bridge, 26
A. Max Brewer Memorial
    Causeway, 26
A. Max Brewer Memorial
    Parkway, 17
Agatized coral, 131
Airbnb, 9, 153, 161
alligator tank, 127
alligators, 25, 29, 46, 48, 63, 77,
    80, 83, 103, 110, 147, 159
Altamonte Springs, 8, 55, 56, 57,
    59, 61, 62, 67, 69, 70, 71, 73, 75,
    79, 81, 83, 85
Altamonte Springs San Sebastian
    Trailhead, 55, 57, 70
American Gothic, 61
American Space Museum, 22
American White Pelicans, 130
Amish Country Store, 140
Anclote. See Anclote River

Anclote River, 115, 116, 117
Anderson Snow Park, 105
Andrews Memorial Chapel,
    126, 129
anhinga, 80
anoles, 80, 148
Anoles, 148, 149
Apollo Program, 30
Apopka Vineland Outpost, 72, 73,
    74, 75
Aripeka, 117
armadillos, 115, 149
Art and Heritage Center, 76
Arts and Crafts, 66
Ashley's Victorian Haven
    B&B, 154
Asia, 25, 66, 111
Asukile, Imani, 102
Atlanta Braves, 69
Atlantic, 1, 7, 18, 19, 26, 30, 32,
    33, 67, 100, 129
Atlantic Ocean, 7, 18, 19, 26, 30,
    32, 33, 67, 129, See Atlantic
Austin Merritt Road, 164
Azalea Park, 139

Bald Eagles, 25, 28, 43, 62
Bargar, Katherine, 180

Index

Barred Owls, 43
Bates, Michael, 165
Bay Lake Trailhead, 163
Bayshore Boulevard, 130, 144
Beach Drive, 144
Beaux-Arts movement, 141
Beck Ranch Park, 36, 37, 38, 41, **42,** 47
Belted Kingfishers, 25
Benoist Plaza, 151
Best Western, 154
Beyond the Wall B&B, 154
bicycle, 2, 5, 6, 7, 8, 13, 15, 19, 22, 23, 26, 33, 34, 35, 44, **47,** 53, 58, 69, 73, 74, 77, 79, 81, 90, 95, 96, 97, 122, 127, 129, 137, 145, 146, 147, 148, 157, 158, 161, 163, 181
Bicycling, 1, 160
bicycling route, 2
bicyclists, 4, 6, 8, 103, 113, 122, 134, 157, 161
Big Freeze, 85
bioluminescent plankton, 27
bison, 12, 149
Black mangroves, 128
Black Point Wildlife Drive, 17, 25, 26
Black Skimmers, 43
Blackwater Cutoff Trail, 108
Blossom Lake Park, 139
Blue Springs, 49, 50, 51, 52
Blue Springs State Park, 49, 50, 51
boat tours, 34, 51
bobcats, 25, 29
Boca Ciega Bay, 147, 148, 149
Boca Ciega Millennium Park, 139, 148, 149
Boggy Bayou, 128

Botanical Gardens, 62, 138, 139, 140, 142, 147
Brazil, 100
Brevard County, 31
Brevard County School Board, 31
Brevard County School Teachers Emeritus, 31
Britton Hill, 82
Brock House, 48
Brooker Creek Preserve, 105, 106, 107, 108, 109, 112, 157, 158
Brooker Creek Preserve and Environmental Education Center, 105, 112
Brooksville, vii, 1, 10, 87, 88, 89, 90, 91, 92, **94,** 94, 95, 96, 97, **101,** 102, 103, 154, 155, 156, 157, 162, 163
Brooksville Quarry Disc Golf Course, 97
Brooksville Ridge, 97
Brotemarkle, Benjamin D, 165
Brown Pelicans, 130
Bryan, Jonathan R, 165
Buddha, **24**
Bushell, 164
Bushnell, 99, 155
butterflies, 81, 110

C2C, 1, 2, **3,** 4, 5, 6, 8, 9, 10, 11, 12, 13, 14, 15, 16, 18, 19, 20, 21, 22, 24, 25, 26, 27, 28, 30, 31, 35, 38, 40, 41, 42, 43, 44, 45, 46, 47, 39, 51, 54, 57, 58, 60, **61,** 62, 63, 66, 69, 72, 73, 74, 76, 78, 79, 80, 81, 83, **84,** 86, 89, 90, 91, 92, 93, 94, 95, 96, 97, 98, 99, 101, 102, 104, 107, 108, 109, 110, 112, 113, 114, 115, 116, 117, 120, 121, 122, 124, 126, 127, 129,

Index

133, 135, 136, 139, 140, 141, 142, 146, 147, 148, 150, 152, 153, 154, 155, 156, 157, 158, 159, 160, 162, 163, 164, 180, *See* C2C Trail

C2C Trail, 1, 10, 12, 13, 15, 20, 40, 49, 89, 90, 104, 107, 112, 121, 146, 160, *See* Coast-to-Coast Trail

Caladesi Island, 129, 135

Canal Street, 31, 33

Cannon, Jeff, 165

Captain Charles Mellon, 66

Captain Mellon. *See* Captain Charles Mellon

Carnegie Library, 142

Carnegie, Andrew, 142

Castillo de San Marcos, 33

Celery City, 64

Celtic Festival, 132

Center Hill, 164

Central Florida, 43, 46, 63, 76, 86, 92, 96, **114,** 131, 157, 159

Central Florida Railroad Museum, 78

Central Florida Zoo & Botanical Gardens, 62

Chain of Lakes Park, 17, 21, 27, 28

Chapin Station, 72, 76

Charles Sumner, 102

Chihuly Collection, 146

Chùa Báo Ân Buddhist Temple, 73

Citrus Label Tour. *See* Lake County Citrus Label Tour

Citrus Springs, 102

Citrus Tower, 14

Clarcona Horse Park, 74, 155

Clark, James C, 165

Clearwater, 118, 119, 120, 122, 131, 133, 135, 138, 140, 147, 148, 154, 155

Clearwater Beach, 118, 121, 122, 133, 135, 137, 154,

Clearwater Beach Pier 122

Clearwater Cleveland Street District, 120

Clearwater Marine Aquarium, 137

Clearwater Memorial Park, 122

Clermont, 4, 14, 70, 72, 74, 75, 76, 79, 81, 82, 85, 87, 89, 90, **91,** 92, 95, 153, 154, 155, 156, 158, 166

Clermont Historic Village Museum, 90

Clermont Historical Village, 92

Clermont Waterfront Park, 70, 72, 76, 79, 82, 87, 90, 95, 158

Cleveland Street, 118, 120, 121, 122, 127, 138

Cleveland Street District, 118, 120, 127, 138

Coachman Park, 120

Coast-to-Coast Trail, 1, 152, 160

Colonel Henry T. Titus, 30

coquina, 33

Corral Parking Lot, 113

Cortez Boulevard/SR 50 Trail, 90

Countryman One Room Schoolhouse, 94

Cowboys, 48

CR469, 164

cracker, 48

Crews Lake Wilderness Park, 110

crocodiles, 63

Croom, 87, 89, 90, 92, 96, 97, 101, 103, 155, 162

Croom MTB Parking 89

Croom Rital Road Trailhead, 89

Croom Wildlife Management
    Area, 87, 90, 92, 96
cycling. *See* Bicycling
cyclists, 1, 3, 6, 7, 8, 9, 10, **28,** 34,
    44, 57, 59, 72, 76, 79, 82, 89,
    122, 134, 162, 163
Cypress Glen Campground, **155**
cypress trees, 46, 94

Dade Battlefield, 98
Dade Battlefield Historic State
    Park, 99
Dade City, 109, 117
Dade Massacre, 99
Dalí Museum, 145
Davis, Jack E, **165**
De León. *See* Juan Ponce de León
DeBary, 36, 38, 40, 41, 42, 44, 45,
    153, 154, 41, 42, 43, 44, 45, 46,
    49, 155, 156, 157, 158
DeBary Hall, 38, 41
DeBary Hall Trailhead, 38
DeLand, 53, 54
DeLeon Springs, 36, 49, 50, 51,
    52, **53**
DeLeon Springs State Park,
    49, 51
Demens. *See* Peter Demens
Depot Museum, 122
Devil in the Grove, 86, 159, 166
Dixie Crossroads, 23
Dodecanese Boulevard, 124
dog parks, 95
Don CeSar Hotel, 152
Downtown Titusville. *See*
    Titusville
ducks, 28
Dunedin, 4, 6, 118, 120, 121, 126,
    127, 129, **132**, 154, 155, 156,
    157, 158

Dunedin Downtown Market, 126
Dunedin History Museum, 126

East Central Regional Rail Trail,
    15, 18, 38
East Coast Surfing Museum, 34
eastern indigo snakes, 116
Eatonville, 159
Edgewater, 19, 31, 33, 77, 127, 153
Edgewater Inn, 77
Education Center, 75, 80, **81**, 105,
    108, 112, 113, 158
Education Center Trail, 108
egrets, 25, 28, 62, 64, 80, 134
Enterprise, 38, 44, 48, 49, 66
Etna Turpentine Camp, 100
Everglades, 63, 64, 159

Farmer's Market Restaurant, 92
Farmton, 25
Farmton Tract, 25
FBI, 31
Federal Armed Occupation Act of
    1842, 133
Ferns, 44
Fish and Wildlife Conservation
    Commission, 114, 165
fishermen, 20, 44, 60, 77, 137
Flagler Avenue, 34
Flagler Avenue Beachfront
    Park, 34
Flamingo, 43
flatwoods ecosystems, 28
Flatwoods Trail, 108
Florida, 1, 3, 4, 5, 6, 7, 9, 10, 11,
    12, **13**, 15, 16, 22, 25, 26, 27, 28,
    29, 30, 31, 33, 34, 35, 41, 43, 44,
    45, 46, 47, 48, 51, 52, 61, 62, 63,
    64, 66, 67, 68, 69, 76, 77, 78, 79,
    81, 82, 83, 85, 86, 91, 92, 95, 96,

97, 98, 99, 100, 102, 103, 104,
110, **111,** 112, **113, 114,** 115,
116, 117, 120, 121, 122, 126,
128, 129, 130, 131, 133, 135,
138, 140, 142, 147, 148, 149,
150, 152, 157, 158, 159, 160,
161, 165, 166, 180, 181
Florida Bicycle Association, 161
Florida black bears, 62, 64, 159
Florida cattle, 48
Florida Citrus Tower, 14, 79
Florida Coast-to-Coast Trail. *See*
Coast-to-Cost Trail; C2C Trail
Florida Collegiate Summer
League, 69
Florida Department of
Environmental Protection,
15, 160
Florida Department of
Transportation, 15, 160
Florida East Coast Railway, 68
Florida Freewheelers Horrible
Hundred, 79
Florida Lakewatch, 83
Florida Native Plant Society,
44, 181
Florida Progressive Voter's
League, 31
Florida Scrub Jay, 26, 82, 116
Florida State Park, 51
Florida State University Digital
Library, 27
Florida Statutes, 7
Florida: Bald Cypress. *See* cypress
trees
Florida's Aquifer, 97, 104
Florida's Office of Greenways and
Trails, 4
Folk Victorian, 66
Fort DeSoto Park, 148

Fort Mellon Park, 57, 59
fox squirrels, 103
Frederick deBary, 42
freshwater, 11, 15, 29, 45, 51, 52,
63, 83, 97, 112, 116, 117, 133
freshwater springs, 11, 45, 51,
116, 133

Gainesville, 102, 149, 165
gallinules, 80
Gandy Bridge, 152
Gannon, Michael, 165
Gap Center Hill Northern
Route, 164
gators. *See* alligators
Gemini Springs North
Trailhead, 38
Gemini Springs Park, 36, 38,
40, 41, 44, **45,** 47, 49, 51, 155,
157, 158
Gilbert King, 86, 159
Gobbler's Lodge Trailhead, 17
Goff, Lauren, 160
Good Neighbor Connector, 90
Good Neighbor Trail, 15, 87, 90,
94, 97, 101, 103, 164
Google Maps, 2, 9, 10, 160
Gopher tortoise, 80, 82, 113, **114,**
115, 116, 129, 135, 147
GPS, 2, 10, 161, 162
Grant Wood, 61
Gray Catbirds, 29
Great Blue Heron, 60
Great Clermont Triathlon, 79
Great Egrets, 25
Great Florida Birding Trail, 28
Greek Orthodox Epiphany,
124, 126
green anole (*Anolis
carolinensis*), 148

Green Springs Park, 38, 40, 41, 44, 49
Green Swamp, 94, 103, 104, 163
Groveland, 1, 10, 85, 86, 89, , 91, 92, 159, 162, 163, 166
Groveland Four, 86
Groveland Museum, 92
Gulf Coast, 109
Gulf of Mexico, 1, 13, 97, 115, 117, 127, 129, 130, 132, 133, **135**, 137, 147

Hammock Park, 120, 121, 126, 129
Hampton Inn, 153, 154
Hancock Road intersection, 74
Harriet Beecher Stowe, 48
Harry and Harriet Moore, 31
Harry T. and Harriet V. Moore Cultural Complex, 30, 31
Haulover Canal Bridge, 26
hawks, 28, 29, 41
Healthy West Orange Arts and Heritage Center, 79, 83
Healthy West Orange Arts and Heritage Center at the Town of Oakland, 79
Heartwood Preserve, 115
Henry S. Sanford, 67
Hensley, Donald, 166
Heritage Museum, 78, 94, 124
Heritage Village, 138, 142, 147, 150, **151**
Hernando. See Hernando County,
Hernando County, 94, **101**, 102, 162, 165
Hernando County, Florida, Black America Series, 102, 165
Hernando de Soto, 130
Hernando Heritage Museum, 94

herons, 28, 60, 62, 64, 80, 134
Hezekiah Osteen, 47
Hiaasen, Carl, 160
Hickory Bluff Preserve, 154
Highland Games Festival, 132
Highway A1A South Causeway, 34
hiking, 6, 8, 10, 16, 40, 46, 51, 52, 75, 77, 80, 97, 99, 110,122, 113, 115, 121, 129, 140, 160
hiking trails, 10, 77, 80, 99, 110, 112, 113, 121, 129, 140
Hillsborough. See Hillsborough River
Historic Brooksville, 87
Historic DeBary Hall, 41
Historic Sanford, 55
Historic Sanford Memorial Stadium, 69
Historic Village, 70, 79, 90, 158
Hog Island Recreation Area, 90, 155
Hog Island Recreation Area and Campground, 90
Holiday Inn, 153, 154
Hollerbach's Willow Tree Café, 69
Honeymoon Island, 118, 127, 129, 131, 133, 134, **135**, 154, 157
Honeymoon Island State Park, 118
Hontoon Island, 12
Hudson, 117
Hurricane Pass, 129, 135
hurricanes, 127, 129, 159
Hurston, Zora Neal, 159

I-4, 9, 19, 40, 55, 57, 58, 59, 60, 66, 69, 153
I-95, 21, 24

Images of America:
  Brooksville, 102
Imani D. Asukile, 102
Indian River, 14, 20, 21, 22, 26, 28, 30, 33, 34
Indian River Lagoon, 28, 34
International Harvester, 25
Interstate 4, 58
Intracoastal Waterway, 30, 33, 136
Inverness, 100, 103

Jacksonville, 14, 30, 67, 68
James McNeill, 117, 165
Jay B. Starkey Wilderness Park, 105, 107, 108, **109,** 113, 115, 116, 117
Jeff Sonksen, 60, **61**
joggers, 60
John James Audubon, 52
John S. Taylor Park, 138, 140
Johnson, Miriam W, 166
Jones Trailhead, 57, 60
Josiah Cephas Weaver Park, 121, 129
Juan Ponce de León, 12

Kambic, Randy, 166
kayaking, 26, 51, 147
kayaking and paddleboard tours, 26
Kennedy Space Center, 22, 23, 154
Key West, 68
Killarney Station, 9, 72, 76, 81
Killarney Station trailhead, 9, 81
King, Gilbert, 86, 159
Kissimmee, 42, 158
KOA, 154, 155
Ku Klux Klan, 31

Lake Apopka, 75, 77, 78, 80, 84, 158
Lake Apopka Restoration Act, 77
Lake Beresford Park, 51, 53
Lake County, 72, 74, 90, 92
Lake County Citrus Label Tour, 92
Lake County Historical Society, 92
Lake Hiawatha Preserve, 87, 90, 95
Lake Mary, 55, 57, 58, 59, 60, 62, 153, 156, 158
Lake Minnehaha, 158
Lake Minneola, 74, 76, 79, 82, 83, **91,** 95, 153
Lake Monroe, 13, 14, 30, 36, 38, 40, 41, 45, 48, 49, 51, 55, 57, 58, **59,** 60, 62, 66, 67, **68,** 69, 84, 154
Lake Monroe Boat Ramp, 44
Lake Monroe Conservation Area, 41
Lake Monroe Sailing Association, 45
Lake Monroe Wayside Park, 55
Lake Tarpon, 112, 155
Lake Wales Ridge, 80, 81, 82, 97
Land O' Lakes, 115, 116
Largo, 138, 139, 140, 142, 147, 150
Largo Central Park, 142
Largo Feed Store & Museum, 142
Limestone, 33, 97, 98, 104, 131, 135
limpkins, 28, 80
Linden, 99, 163
Live Oak, 41, 95, 96
llamas, 149
Long Bayou, 147

long-distance walks, 5
Longwood, 41, 57, 60
Lulu Creek Trail, 74
Lyft, 89

Mabel, 99, 163
Magnificent Frigatebirds, 43
Major Francis Dade, 99
Mammoths, 149
Manasota, 150
manatees, 25, 26, 32, 52, 123, 124
Mangrove forests, 128
Mangroves, 128, 129
Map My Ride, 10, 161, 162,
    163, 164
Marine Discovery Center, 34
Martinez, Robert, 102, **166**
Masaryktown, 110
Mascotte, 91, 92
Mascotte Civic Center, 92
Mayaca, 48
May-Stringer House, 94
Maytown, 17, 19, 21, 25, **28**,
    31, 35
Maytown Spur Trailhead, 17,
    21, 25
McNeill Homestead, 117
McPhee, John, 160
Mellonville, 66, 67
Memorial Causeway Bike Trail,
    135, 136
Meranova B&B, 154
mermaid, 95
Merritt Island, 17, 20, 22, 23, 25,
    26, 157
Merritt Island National Wildlife
    Refuge, 22, 25, 157
Merritt Island NWR Visitor
    Center, 26
Miami Corporation, 25

Mims, 24, 25, 28, 30, 158
Minneola Scenic Trail, 72, 74
Minneola Trailhead Park, 72, 76
Mirror Lake, 141
Mirror Lake Community
    Library, 141
Mockingbird, 43
Monroe Harbor Marina, 59
Moores, 30, 31
Morean Arts Center, 146
Mosquito County, 83
Mosquito Lagoon. Paddlers, 27
mosquitos, 83, 159
Mural Project, 122
Museum of Fine Arts, 146
Museum of Natural History, 149

NAACP, 31
NASA, 22, 26, 30
National Advancement of
    Colored People, 31, *See*
    NAACP
National Register of Historic
    Places, 21, 66, 93, 126, 152
National Training Center, 79
Nelson, Gill, **166**
Nestlé, 116
New Smyrna. *See* New Smyrna
    Beach
New Smyrna Beach, 17, 19, 31,
    33, 34, 35,
New Smyrna Beach Museum of
    History, 34
New Smyrna Beach's Canal Street
    district, 31
New York City, 110
New York Giants, 69
Newton Park, 77, 80
Nobleton, **90**, **163**, **164**
North Causeway, 34

North Florida, 46, 104
Northern Cardinals, 29

Oakland, 70, 72, 75, 76, 77, **78**, 79, 80, **81,** 83, 84, 16, 157, 158,
Oakland Nature Preserve, 70, 75, 76, 77, 80, **81,** 157, 158
Ocala Limestone Formation, 97
Ocklawaha. *See* Ocklawaha River
Ocoee, 73, 74, 83, 86
Ocoee Massacre, 86
Old Fort Park, 33
Old Jailhouse, 69
Old Spanish Sugar Mill restaurant, 52, **53**
Open Air Post Office, 152
Orange Belt Railway, **13**, 67, 76, 84, 123, 132, 133, 150, 152
Orange County, 1, 61, 72, 83, 84, 166
Orlando, 42, 61, 72, 83, 158, 166, 182
Orleans, Susan, 160
Osprey, 25, 43, 60, 62, 80, 130, 134
Osteen, 14, 17, 19, 21, 25, 27, 28, **29**, 36, 38, 40, 41, 44, 47
Osteen Civic Center, 17, 19, 36, 38, 40, 41
Osteen Civic Center trailhead, 17, 36, 38, 41
owls, 29

paddleboard, 26
Paint the Trail, 55, 60, **61**
Palatka, 68
Palm Court Motel, 154
Palm Harbor, 120, 126, 127
Pánfilo de Narváez, 130
panniers, **7,** 8

Parrish Park, 17, 19, 20, 26
Pasco. *See* Pasco County
Pasco County, 109, 116, 166
Patrick D. Smith, 48, 159
pelicans, 43, 130, 137, 140
Peter Demens, **13**, 84, 150
Petrovitch A. Demenscheff. *See* Peter Demens
picnic facilities, 110, 126, 127, 142
picnicking, 51
Pinellas County, **13**, 15, 85, 107, 112, 118, 120, 122, 129, 130, 131, 138, 142, 148, 150, **151**, 152
Pinellas County Bicycle Advisory Committee, 15
Pinellas Point Temple Mound, 150
Pinellas Trail, 2, 15, 120, 122, 140, 141, 152
Pithlachascotee. *See* Pithlachascotee River
Pithlachascotee River, 115
play areas, 110, 140
Playa Linda Beach, 19
Pleistocene, 82, 149
Poinciana, 42, 158
Ponce de Leon, 12, 53
Pond Cypress. *See* cypress trees
Pop Stansell Park, 126
Port Richey, 105, 107, 113, 115, 117
Pratts, J. J., 166
President Grover Cleveland, 49
President Ulysses S. Grant, 48
Preston Brooks, 102
primitive camping, 97, 110
Princess Martha Hotel, 152
Pritchard House, 21

racoons, 110
railway museum, 110
Rawlings, Marjorie Kinnan, 160
Red mangroves, 128
Red-cockaded Woodpeckers,
    113, 116
Red-shouldered Hawks, 43
region west of Mims, 25
remote walk, 21
Reséndez, Andrés, 130, 160, 166
Residence Inn, 154
Richloam, 92, **93**, 96, 163
Richloam General Store, **93**
Richloam Wildlife Management
    Area, 92, 96, 163
Richloam WMA, 163
Ride with GPS, 10, 161, 162
Robbins Manufacturing
    Company, 99
Robert Martinez, 102
Robison, Jim, 166
rose mallow. *See* swamp hibiscus
Roseate Spoonbill, 25, 43,
    135, 138
Russell Street Park, 89, 90, 94
Russell, Karen, 160

Sabal Palm, **111**
Safety Harbor, 12, 150
Safety Harbor Temple
    Mound, 150
Safford Avenue, 120, 122
Safford House Museum, 124
Saint Joseph Sound, 134
Saint Nicholas Greek Orthodox
    Cathedral, 120, **121**
saltwater, 63
Salvador Dalí Museum, 145
San Sebastian Trailhead, 55, 57,
    60, 70, 72

Sand Point Park, 22
Sanford, 9, 13, 36, 38, 42, 45, 55,
    57, 58, **59**, 60, 61, 62, 64, 66, 67,
    68, 69, 76, 84, 153, 156, 157
Sanford Marina, 60, **68**
Sanford Spur Trail, 36, 57, 60, 62
Sanford's Historic District, 69
Sanlando Park, 57, 61
Sanlando Softball Complex, 61
Saturday Morning Market, 146
Saturn V rockets, 23
Scottish American Society, 132
Sears, 66
Second Seminole War, 66
sedimentary rock, 97, 131
Seminole City Park, 139, 148
Seminole County, 12, 38, 55, 61,
    62, 64
Seminole Softball Complex, 57
Seminole Tribe, 11, 12, 66, 98,
    99, 131
Seminole Wars, 12, 98, 99
Seminole Wekiva Trail, 2, **3**, 15,
    55, 57, 58, 60, 70, 72,
Seminoles. *See* Seminole Tribe
Serenova Tract, 115
Seven Springs, 117
Sheriff Willis McCall, 86
Shuttle Launch Experience, 23
Sibley, David Allen, 166
Silver Lake Campground, 90
Silver Lake/Crooked River
    Campground, 155
sinkhole, 46, 116
skating, 79
Snail Kites, 80
Snowy Egrets, 64
Sonksen. *See* Jeff Sonksen
South America, 111
South Carolina, 102

South Lake Trail, 15, 72, 74, 90
South Riverside Drive, 33
Southwest Florida, 48, 115
Southwest Florida Water
  Management District, 115
Space View Park, 20, 21, 22, **23**
SpaceX, 30
Spanish moss, 41, 96
Sponge Diving, 124, 132, 157
sponge docks, 115, 118, 120, 124,
  125, 157
sponges, 14, 125
Spring Bayou, 120, 123, 124, 132
Spring Bayou Live Manatee
  Webcam, 124
Spring Garden Run, 53
Spring Hill, 87, 105, 110, 154, 156
Spring Hill African American
  Cemetery, 102
Spring Training, 69
Springhill, 89, 105, 153, 156
Spring-to-Spring Trail, 36, 38, 40,
  46, 49, 51, 53, 54, 58,
spur trail, 10, 17, 19, 31, 36, 40,
  41, 49, 51, 55, 57, 58, 59, 60, 62,
  66, 73, 74, 87, 92, 102, 103, 118,
  121, 127, 129, 133, 135, 156
squirrels, 103, 110, 159
SR 50, 19, 87, 89, 90, 95, 96, 98,
  103, 104, 105, 108, 109, 154,
  155, 156, 162, 163, 164
SR 50 Sumter/Lake County
  trail, 90
SR 50 Trailhead, 87, 89, 95,
  103, 105
SR33, 164
SR48, 164
St. Augustine, 33
St. John's River-to-Sea Loop, 19

St. Johns River, 13, 14, 27, 29, 30,
  35, 38, 41, 44, 48, 57, 62, 64, 67
St. Johns Rivership Co., 68
St. Nicholas Cathedral, 124
St. Pete Pier, 141, 142, **144**, 151
St. Petersburg, 1, 2, 9, 13, 76, 85,
  123, 138, 139, 140, **141**, **144**,
  145, 146, 147, 148, 150, 151,
  152, 154, 155, 156, 157, 158
Starkey Boulevard Trail, 107
Starkey Environmental Education
  Center, 113
Starkey Park Bike Trailhead, 107
Starkey Wilderness, 105, 107, 108,
  109, 113, 155
Starkey Wilderness Park
  Trail, 109
State of Florida, 4, 31, 82, 86, 95,
  103, 114, 180
State of Oklahoma, 98
Station Square Park, 133
steamboats, 14, 48, 68
Stetson University, 53
Strava, 10, 162
Sugarloaf Mountain, 82
Sulphur Springs, 151
Sumner. *See* Charles Sumner
Sumter. *See* Sumter County, *See*
  Sumter County
Sumter County, 99
Suncoast Parkway, 87, 89, 90,
  95, 105, 108, 109, 110, 115,
  154, 156
Suncoast Trail, 15, 89, 90, 105,
  107, 108
Suncoast Trail SR 50
  Trailhead, 89
Suncoast Trail State Road 50
  Trailhead, 105
SunRail, 42, 44, 157, 158

SunRail station, 42, 44
Sunshine State, 11
Swallow-tailed Kites, 29, 43
swamp hibiscus, 80
swamp mallow, 80
Swap-O-Rama Webster Westside Flea Market, 92
swimming, 27, 44, 51, 52, 63, 83

Tampa, 14, 99, 112, 113, 129, 130, 131, 140, **144,** 145, 149, 150, 151, 152, 160
Tampa Bay, 99, 112, 113, 129, 130, 131, 140, **144,** 145, 149, 150, 160
Tarpon Avenue, 120, 122
Tarpon Springs, 14, 105, 107, 108, 112, 115, 118, 120, **121,**122, 123, 124, **125,** 126, 128, 129, 132, 154, 155, 156, 157, 166
Tarpon Springs Aquarium, 124
Tarrytown, 92, 96, 99, 104
Taylorville. See Groveland
Tebeau, Charlton, 166
terns, 43
The Florida Greenways and Trails System, 15
Thornby Park, 40
Timucuan, 78
Titus House, 30
Titusville, 1, 2, 4, 9, 14, 17, 19, 20, 21, 22, **23,** 25, 26, 27, 30, 154, 155, 156, 157, 158
Titusville Welcome Center, 17, 19, 23
Tocobaga, 130, 150
Tocobaga Tribe, 150
Tomáš Masaryk, 110
tortoises, 80, 82, 113, **114,** 115, 116, 129, 135, 147, 149, 159

Trailhead Park, 72, 73, 76, 139
Tri-County Trail, 15, 107
Trilby, 102, 103, 163
Trinity/Odessa, 154
Tropical Inn, 154
Truman Scarborough Way, 17, 21, 27, 28
turkeys, 103, 115
turpentine, 81, 85, 92, 93, 99, 100
turtles, 80, 137

Uber, 89
US 1, 33
US Senate Chamber, 102
US Senator Charles Sumner, 102
US space program, 30

Van Fleet Trail, 87, 103, 163
Veterans' Memorial Park, 59
Vinoy Renaissance Hotel, 141
Virginia, 100
Volusia County, 25, 38, 41, 49
Volusia Forever, 41

walkers, 1, 2, 3, 4, 6, 7, 8, 21, 44, 60, 76, 90, 108, 121, 122, 134, 137, 157, 158
walking, 1, 2, 4, 6, 8, 10, 16, 26, 30, 33, 40, 60, 69, 75, 79, 95, 120, 121, 127, 142, 145
Wall Springs Park, 118, 120, 127, 128, 157
Walsingham Park, 139, 140, 147
warblers, 28, 48, 129
Warmshowers, 9, 161
Washington Avenue, 21, 30
Watch Discovery Center, 145
Water Management District. See, See Southwest Florida Water Management District

Waterfront Park. *See* Clermont
  Waterfront Park
Wayside Park, 36, 38, 41, 55,
  57, 58
Webster, 87, 92, 93, 96, 163
Weeden Island, 12, 130, 150
Weedon Island Mounds, 150
Weedon Island Preserve, 150
Weeki Wachee Springs, 95
Weeki Wachee Springs State
  Park, 95
West Orange Trail, 9, 15, 72, 73,
  74, 75, 76, 79, **84**
West Orange Trail Bikes &
  Blades, 9
West Orange Trail Winter
  Garden Station, 75
West Pasco Audubon Society, 115
White Ibises, 29
White mangroves, 128
White pelicans, 130
White Sands Buddhist Center,
  21, **24**, 158
White, Randy Wayne, 160
white-tailed deer, 103, 115
Wild Persimmon hiking trail
  loop, 52
Wild Turkey, 29, 96, 115
Wilderness Trail, 107, 108
wildfires, 112
Wildlife Management Area.
  See Richloam Wildlife
  Management Area

William A. Edwards, 102
William Bartram, 52
Windover, 12, 27
Windover Archeological Site, 27
Winter Garden, 4, 6, 70, 72, 74,
  75, 76, 77, 80, 83, 85, 153, 155,
  156, 157, 158
Winter Garden Heritage
  Foundation, 77
Winter Garden Station, 72, 74,
  75, 76
Winter Garden Station
  Trailhead, 74
Winter Park, 42, 158
Wise, Madonna Jervis, **166**
Withlacoochee. *See*
  Withlacoochee River
Withlacoochee River, 97, 101, 155
Withlacoochee State Forest,
  96, 157
Withlacoochee State Trail, 10,
  100, 102
Withlacoochee Trail, 87, 89, 90,
  92, 96, 101, 103, 162, 163

Withlacoochee Trailhead, 87, 92
woodpeckers, 28, 29, 80, 113, 116

Youth Camp Road, 164

Zephyrhills, 116, 117

ACKNOWLEDGMENTS

Thank you to the many trail advocates who work hard to create shared-use trails, and to the individuals working for municipalities and the State of Florida whose efforts helped to establish the C2C. Thank you to all of those who supported me in the research and writing of this book, and who gave me encouragement along the way, including author Mark I. Pinksy for his editing guidance, and to Stuart Beal and Lisa Portelli for their Florida cycling expertise and advice. Thank you to Elizabeth Crowell for the many hours she spent editing this work and encouraging me, and for her brilliant insights and cheerful assistance. Kathy Bargar is an excellent photographer and I appreciate her artistic capabilities, hard work, and organizational skills. Her work was essential to the creation of this book. Finally, profound thanks to my husband and bicycling partner, Don Crowell, whose support has made this book possible and who is always ready for an adventure.

ABOUT THE AUTHOR

Nanci J. Adler is a longtime cyclist and avid bicycle tourist, having explored the United States and over 10 countries on multiweek, self-supported bicycle tours along with her husband. Her love of bicycling inspired her thesis *The Bicycle in Western Literature: Transformations on Two Wheels* for her master's degree in Liberal Studies at Rollins College. Her essay "The Existential Cyclist" was published in the anthology *Culture on Two Wheels*, University of Nebraska Press. A Florida resident since 1981, Ms. Adler is also an advocate for protecting wildlife and the natural environment. She is a UF/IFAS Florida Master Naturalist, a member of the Florida Native Plant Society, and a longtime volunteer at the Audubon Center for Birds of Prey in Maitland, Florida. Ms. Adler lives in Maitland, Florida, with her husband, Don Crowell.

ABOUT THE PHOTOGRAPHER

Katherine Bargar, of Orlando, Florida, is a retired graphic designer, photographer, and recreational cyclist. She has participated in many weeklong cycling events around the United States and appreciates that the increase of paved bike trails makes it much more enjoyable and safer to ride. As an avid photographer and outdoor enthusiast, she is passionate about traveling to photograph nature and landscape subjects.